MULTICULTURAL EDUCATION SERIES

James A. Banks, Series Editor

Learning and Not Learning English

Latino Students in American Schools

Guadalupe Valdés

Teachers College, Columbia University
New York and London

To my mother,

Ninfa Theobald de Valdés,

Who first introduced me to the pleasures and problems of bilingualism

Published by Teachers College Press, 1234 Amsterdam Avenue, New York, NY 10027

Copyright © 2001 by Teachers College, Columbia University

Library of Congress Cataloging-in-Publication Data

Valdés, Guadalupe.
    Learning and not learning English : Latino students in American schools / Guadalupe Valdés.
        p. cm. — (Multicultural education series)
    Includes bibliographical references and index.
    ISBN 0-8077-4106-X (cloth : alk. paper) — ISBN 0-8077-4105-1 (pbk. : alk. paper)
        1. English language—Study and teaching—Spanish speakers.   2. English
    language—Study and teaching—United States.   3. Hispanic Americans—Education.
    4. Bilingualism—United States.   I. Title.   II. Multicultural education series (New York, N.Y.)
    PE1129.S8 V26 2001
    428′.0071′073—dc21   00-054495

ISBN 0-8077-4105-1 (paper)
ISBN 0-8077-4106-X (cloth)

Printed on acid-free paper

Manufactured in the United States of America

08 07 06 05 04 03   8 7 6 5 4 3

Contents

Series Foreword

The nation's deepening ethnic texture, interracial tension and conflict, and the increasing percentage of students who speak a first language other than English make multicultural education imperative in the 21st century. The U.S. Bureau of the Census estimated that people of color made up 28% of the nation's population in 2000 (U.S. Bureau of the Census, 1998). The Census predicts that their numbers will grow to 38% of the nation's population in 2025 and 47% in 2050.

American classrooms are experiencing the largest influx of immigrant students since the beginning of the 20th century. About a million immigrants are making the United States their home each year (Martin & Midgley, 1999). More than seven and one-half million legal immigrants settled in the United States between 1991 and 1998, most of whom came from nations in Latin America and Asia (Riche, 2000). A large but undetermined number of undocumented immigrants also enter the United States each year. The influence of an increasingly ethnically diverse population on the nation's schools, colleges, and universities is and will continue to be enormous.

In 1998, 34.9 percent of the students enrolled in U.S. public schools were students of color; this percentage is increasing each year, primarily because of the growth in the percentage of Latino students (Martinez & Curry, 1999). In some of the nation's largest cities and metropolitan areas, such as Chicago, Los Angeles, Washington, D.C., New York, Seattle, and San Francisco, half or more of the public school students are students of color. During the 1998–1999 school year, students of color made up 63.1% of the student population in the public schools of California, the nation's largest state (California State Department of Education, 2000).

Language diversity is also increasing among the nation's student population. Sixteen percent of school-age youth in 1990 lived in homes in which English was not the first language spoken (U.S. Bureau of the Census, 1998). Most teachers now in the classroom and in teacher education programs are likely to have students from diverse ethnic, racial, and language groups in their classrooms during their careers. This is true for both inner-city and suburban teachers.

An important goal of multicultural education is to improve race relations and to help all students acquire the knowledge, attitudes, and skills needed to participate in cross-cultural interactions and in personal, social, and civic action that will help make our nation more democratic and just. Multicultural education is consequently as important for middle-class White suburban students as it is for students of color who live in the inner city. Multicultural education fosters the public good and the overarching goals of the commonwealth.

The major purpose of the *Multicultural Education Series* is to provide preservice educators, practicing educators, graduate students, and scholars with an interrelated and comprehensive set of books that summarizes and analyzes important research, theory, and practice related to the education of ethnic, racial, cultural, and language groups in the United States and the education of mainstream students about diversity. The books in the *Series* provide research, theory, and practical knowledge about the behaviors and learning characteristics of students of color, language minority students, and low-income students. They also provide knowledge about ways to improve academic achievement and race relations in educational settings.

The definition of multicultural education in the *Handbook of Research on Multicultural Education* (Banks & Banks, 1995) is used in the *Series*: "multicultural education is a field of study designed to increase educational equity for all students that incorporates, for this purpose, content, concepts, principles, theories, and paradigms from history, the social and behavioral sciences, and particularly from ethnic studies and women studies" (p. xii). In the *Series*, as in the *Handbook*, multicultural education is considered a "metadiscipline."

The dimensions of multicultural education, developed by Banks (1995) and described in the *Handbook of Research on Multicultural Education*, provide the conceptual framework for the development of the books in the *Series*. They are: *content integration, the knowledge construction process, prejudice reduction, an equity pedagogy,* and *an empowering school culture and social structure.* To implement multicultural education effectively, teachers and administrators must attend to each of these five dimensions. They should use content from diverse groups when teaching concepts and skills, help students to understand how knowledge in the various disciplines is constructed, help students to develop positive intergroup attitudes and behaviors, and modify their teaching strategies so that students from different racial, cultural, language, and social-class groups will experience equal educational opportunities. The total environment and culture of the school must also be transformed so that students from diverse groups will experience equal status in the culture and life of the school.

Although the five dimensions of multicultural education are highly interrelated, each requires deliberate attention and focus. Each book in the series focuses on one or more of the dimensions, although each book deals with all of them to some extent because of their highly interrelated characteristics.

In this compassionately written, powerful, and insightful study of four students who struggle to learn English while maintaining their dignity, Guadalupe Valdés makes a valuable and singular contribution to the literature on second language learning. This book is unique in part because Valdés is an insider whose observations of Elisa, Manolo, Bernardo, and Lilian evoke painful memories of her own experiences of struggling to learn English when she was a Mexican child in an English-speaking school in the United States.

Valdés' childhood memories are a source of keen insights and empathy. Her own life as a student learning a second language enables her to make powerful and astute observations and recommendations. Like Kenneth B. Clark (1965), the African American psychologist who studied a Harlem Black community, Valdés cannot be a fully detached scholar while studying students whose experience mirror her own life. Both she and Clark are "involved observers" of people in communities like those in which they were socialized. Important studies like this one by Valdés and Clark's *Dark Ghetto* are remarkable because they combine the powerful insights of social scientists with the caring of committed individuals whose projects are to create a better and more humane world. Clark writes convincingly about the shortcomings of scientific detachment and indifference and the need for social scientists to become involved observers:

> On the grounds of absolute objectivity or on a posture of scientific detachment and indifference, a truly relevant and serious social science cannot ask to be taken seriously by a society desperately in need of moral and empirical guidance in human affairs. (p. xxi)

This book also makes an important contribution to the quest for objectivity in the social sciences. By making her value claims and the aims of her research explicit—which is to improve second language teaching and learning for immigrant students—Valdés contributes to both social science research and educational practice. As Myrdal (1969) astutely points out, objectivity in social science research can be attained only if we "expose . . . valuations to full light, make them conscious, specific, and explicit . . . "

(pp. 55–56). When researchers make their value claims explicit, they contribute to what Harding (1991) calls "strong objectivity" because they enable consumers of their work to view it within the context of their life experiences, assumptions, and goals (Banks, 1998).

Today the U.S. is "desperately in need of moral and empirical guidance" in the formulation of a humane policy to guide the education of language minority students. Policy and practice related to the education of these students are too frequently dictated by political expediency rooted in ignorance and fear. The rich and thick descriptions of students and teachers struggling in the ESL classroom described in this significant book reveal the complexity of the problem of second language teaching and learning and can contribute to more enlightened public discourses, policies, and practices.

James A. Banks
Series Editor

REFERENCES

Banks, J. A. (1995). Multicultural education: Historical development, dimensions, and practice. In J. A. Banks & C. A. M. Banks (Eds.), *Handbook of research on multicultural education* (pp. 3–24). New York: Macmillan.

Banks, J. A. (1998). The lives and values of researchers: Implications for educating citizens in a multicultural society. *Educational Researcher, 27*(7), 4–17.

Banks, J. A. & Banks, C. A. M. (Eds.). (1995). *Handbook of research on multicultural education.* New York: Macmillan.

California State Department of Education (2000). [On line.] Available at web site: http://data1.cde.ca.gov/dataquest

Clark, K. B. (1965). *Dark ghetto: Dilemmas of social power.* New York: Harper.

Harding, S. (1991). *Whose science? Whose knowledge? Thinking from women's lives.* Ithaca, NY: Cornell University Press.

Martin, P. & Midgley, E. (1999). Immigration to the United States. *Population Bulletin, 54*(2), 1–44. Washington, D.C.: Population Reference Bureau.

Martinez, G. M. & Curry, A. E. (1999, September). *Current population reports: School enrollment—social and economic characteristics of students* (update). Washington, D.C.: U.S. Census Bureau.

Myrdal, G. (1969). *Objectivity in social research.* New York: Pantheon Books.

Riche, M. F. (2000). America's diversity and growth: Signposts for the 21st century. *Population Bulletin, 55*(2), 1–43. Washington, D.C.: Population Reference Bureau.

United States Census Bureau. (1998). *Statistical abstract of the United States* (118th edition). Washington, D.C.: U.S. Government Printing Office.

Acknowledgments

I want, first of all, to thank the four young people who were the focus of this study and whom I have called Manolo, Elisa, Lilian, and Bernardo. I am grateful that they allowed me into their lives and shared with me their experiences of learning English. I am especially grateful for the generosity with which they tolerated my questions as newly arrived youngsters and for their trust and continuing friendship as young adults.

I also want to thank my mother, Ninfa Theobald de Valdés, for what Einar Haugen (1969) in the dedication of his book *The Norwegian Language in America* (p. vii) called the "pleasures and problems of bilingualism." Like Haugen's parents, my mother gave me and my sisters the gift of two languages and the opportunity to play roles in two worlds rather than one.

I am deeply indebted to the school administrators who supported my study and the teachers who allowed me into their classrooms. I understand how difficult it was for them to have a researcher present during such an extended period of time. I wish that it were possible for me to thank each of them by name.

I owe a special thanks to Rosa Isela Rodríguez, now a faculty member at the University of Texas at El Paso. I am thankful that she agreed to work as the research assistant for the project in spite of the distance to the research site. I appreciate her willingness to leave home at dawn, endure morning traffic congestion, and cheerfully transcribe hours of classroom interaction. I am grateful for her careful work, her extraordinary insights, and her deep interest in the writing of English-language learners. I learned much from her in the course of this project and look forward to working with her again in the future.

The support of the Center for the Study of Writing at the University of California–Berkeley, under the direction of Sarah Freedman, was invaluable. I am especially grateful for her comments on the final report for the project. I have built directly on those comments in revising the report to prepare this book.

It is a special privilege for me to have this book included in the Multi-cultural Education Series under the general editorship of James Banks. I am especially indebted to Jim because, by inviting me to present the DeWitt Wallace–Readers' Digest Distinguished Lecture during his year as president of AERA, he offered me the opportunity to talk to a large audience about the challenges and frustrations encountered by immigrant students in learning English. Without his invitation, the final report for the study on which this book is based might have remained buried away and forgotten. I am grateful for his advice and for his deep concern about second-language learners.

Finally, I am indebted to my adult children, Luis Roberto and Patricia Elena, to my younger children, Nelson and Gia, and to my husband, Bernard Gifford, who at times patiently and at other times less patiently supported both my intensive involvement in the original study and the many days and hours spent in writing and rewriting the final manuscript.

Introduction

Immigrant Children in Schools

Two and a half years after arriving in the United States from Honduras, Elisa Lara wrote the following text. Enrolled in a regular English class—that is, not an English-as-a-second-language (ESL) class—at the ninth-grade level, she had been asked to recount an experience using strong descriptive language.

Flight

> When I was leaving Honduras I remembed I was walking on the side walk to get on the plain, I remenbered I could smell gasoline with smoke, all I could taste was a salty water on my mouth, I could hear the people screaming good bye and the sound of the airplain as I walked in the airplain and touched the shakey seats made me so nervous. and as I saw all my friends and parents waiving at me goodbye. Thats a moment I will always remenbered.
> Remember.

Elisa had made a great deal of progress. She spoke English with confidence, and she even wrote poetry in this language to a secret love. She was serious about school and asked many questions about going to college.

Lilian Duque, a classmate of Elisa's, was very different. Two years after arriving in this country, she was still in the lowest levels of ESL classes and was not enrolled in any "regular" or mainstream courses in any other subjects. She could produce very little English in spoken or written form. At school, she was angry, rebellious and ready to take on the world.

IMPETUS FOR THE STUDY

This book examines the learning of English in American schools by immigrant children. It focuses on the realities that such youngsters face in trying to acquire English in settings in which they interact exclusively with other non-English-speaking youngsters during the entire schoolday. It is designed to fill a gap in the existing literature on non-English-background youngsters by offering a glimpse of the challenges and difficulties faced by Elisa, Manolo, Bernardo, and Lilian, four middle school students who enrolled in schools in the United States for the first time when they were 12 or 13 years old. It is my purpose here to use these youngsters' lives and experiences as a lens through which to examine both the policy and the instructional dilemmas that now surround the education of immigrant children in this country.

The study on which this book is based was funded by the National Center for the Study of Writing at the University of California–Berkeley and had as its purpose examining how children who arrive in this country with what I call "zero" English learn to write in English. My interest was fueled by what I perceived to be another trend in American education that had not totally taken into account the needs of non-English-background students. Very specifically, I worried that the new emphasis on writing across the curriculum might serve as a gatekeeper for these students and that certain policies—including those requiring them to take high school competency exams in which writing is weighted heavily—might produce an even greater number of high school dropouts. What I wanted to know was: How does writing develop in second-language learners, how long does it take, and is it realistic to expect that at some point between, say, sixth grade and high school graduation, second-language learners who arrive here as young teens will be able to write like native speakers of English? Implicit in my questions was a deep concern about the academic success and failure of newly arrived immigrant students.

As it turned out, in closely shadowing four students over a 2-year period, I was able to see many things that had little to do with the development of writing but that in more important ways answered the larger questions I was asking about minority students and their success and failure in schools. This book, then, while it includes much about the development of written language abilities, is not a book primarily about writing. It is, rather, a book about the challenges of learning English. It is also a book about the ways that power is manifested in the choices that are made for students who do not speak English. Finally, it is a book about two hands clapping, that is, about how immigrant children and schools *together* collude to bring about what Kohl (1991) has referred to as *not-learning*. Not

to be confused with failure, *not-learning* is perhaps a milder, less oppositional form of resistance as described by Willis (1977) and Foley (1990).
Kohl (1991) defines the process as follows:

> In the course of my teaching career I have seen children choose to not-learn
> many different skills, ideas, attitudes, opinions, and values. At first I confused
> not-learning with failing. . . . But there were many cases I came upon where
> obviously intelligent students were beyond success or failure when it came to
> reading or other school related learning. They had consciously placed them-
> selves outside the entire system that was trying to coerce or seduce them into
> learning and spent all their time and energy in the classroom devising ways of
> not-learning, short-circuiting the business of failure altogether. . . .
>
> For some not-learning was a strategy that . . . helped them build a small,
> safe world in which their feelings of being rejected by family and society could
> be softened. Not-learning played a positive role and enabled them to take con-
> trol of their lives and get through difficult times. (pp. 16, 20)

In this book, then, I examine and describe the different expressions
that both learning and not-learning English took among four different
youngsters. In the chapters that follow, I talk about the strategies that four
children chose as a means of "surviving" in school. I examine what surviving appeared to mean for the different youngsters, and I describe how they
functioned in a school setting. I examine what learning English meant to
them and what it meant for school personnel. Finally, I describe the options, the opportunities, and the barriers that they encountered.

This is neither a happy nor a comforting book. It is not a book about
successes. It does not fall within the currently popular genre of books on
education that look for examples of best practices and everyday heroes.
This book is about challenges and even about educational dead ends. It is
a book that tells the story of four young people who arrived in middle
school eager to learn and who encountered a school environment that in
some significant ways failed to meet their needs.

There are those who would argue that books such as this should not
be written. They point out that, in spite of their faults, schools are doing
the best that they can under very difficult circumstances. Teachers are un-
derpaid; schools are overcrowded; and population shifts—especially the
influx of new immigrants—have made teaching a very complex endeavor
indeed. They believe that little is to be gained by "school and teacher bash-
ing" and point out that what is needed are examples of good programs
and good teaching that less successful practitioners can imitate.

I have much sympathy for this perspective. It is not my intention in
writing this book to criticize specific teachers or specific schools. The teachers that I write about here were, without question, people of goodwill who

were doing their jobs as best they knew how. They faced extraordinarily difficult problems for which they were not prepared by either their training or their previous experience. They are not to be faulted.

Nevertheless, children in schools today face serious problems. Immigrant children, in particular, present a serious challenge to our existing ideologies about schools' ability to alter the structure of social inequality in this country. While Marxist analyses of schooling in America (e.g., Bowles & Gintis, 1977) have argued that schools simply reproduce the prevailing relations of production and serve to persuade working-class children that their place remains at the bottom, these arguments are neither well known nor accepted by the general public. Many believe that immigrant students fail in school in spite of the best efforts of their schools and their teachers.

What I hope to suggest here is that, like other students who fail, immigrant students are involved in a complex process to which, as Persell (1977) pointed out, numerous forces contribute. Placing blame is not simple. Structures of dominance in society interact with educational structures and educational ideologies as well as with teachers' expectations and with students' perspectives about options and opportunities.

The problems that this book illustrates go far beyond a single school, school district, or even particular area of the country. I use a particular school setting in order to attempt to respond to a single question that I believe is central to our understanding of immigrant students' success or failure in school. It is my intention to attempt to answer the question that I posed about non-English-background students by describing in some detail the everyday school lives of four youngsters, the assumptions about their needs made by the schools they attended, and the children's responses to what was expected of them in the American context.

The view of the four youngsters and of their school experiences that I present in this book is unquestionably a limited one. I brought both to my research and to the interpretation of that research particular values, beliefs, and assumptions. I make no claims to objectivity. Rather, I claim to bring to my description of events, interactions, and dilemmas the perspective of a Mexican woman who, like the youngsters I shadowed during a 2-year period, encountered English for the first time at school. Like my focal students, I arrived at school as a competent speaker of Spanish. I was incompetent only in terms of my ability to use English to present myself authentically as an intelligent and capable young person. Over the course of a lifetime, I have struggled to acquire an authentic English voice.

At the time that I began this study, I had spent a number of years in California, where I had moved from the U.S.–Mexican border. I had spent nearly 15 years studying English–Spanish bilingualism among Mexican immigrant populations. By 1991, when this study began, I had learned much about the Mexican immigrant population away from the border, but I had also found that what I had learned about Mexican immigrants in New Mexico and Texas was very much in evidence in northern California. Far from the border, however, families had broken many ties. Some families had no other relatives in the area, no family networks, no sources of what I have elsewhere called *collective wisdom* (Valdés, 1996). Families struggled on a daily basis to provide for their children; however, in California the stakes appeared to be much higher and the dangers much greater. It was not as easy for new immigrants to give up and to return home.

In a number of ways, much of my own personal and family history became intertwined with this study. English and the learning of English have been a theme in my life for a very long time. My mother, for example, to whom English was very important, still vividly recalls the shame and humiliation she felt when she first arrived in the United States. Placed in a first-grade classroom at the age of 13, she sat among 6-year-old children at a desk that was too small and struggled desperately to maintain her dignity.

My own experience in learning English at the age of 5 was undoubtedly much less painful. I grew up on the border, where I experienced not a metaphorical contact of cultures but a local and particularistic one in which boundaries between communities and between nations were very real. After marrying my father, who had established his medical practice on the Mexican side of the border, my mother moved back to Mexico. Our everyday lives, however, were lived partly in each of the two countries. My sister and I crossed the border every day to attend school in the neighboring Texas city where we used English to read, write, and pray in an all-girls Catholic school among Irish American nuns and Anglophone children. At the end of the day, we crossed the border again and returned to our totally Mexican world.

I was successful at school and in many ways grew to take pride in my competent bilingualism. The memory of my first day at school, however, has remained painfully vivid. I remember the classroom and the rows of seated children. I recall that my teacher, a young and pretty nun, spoke to me in a gentle voice. I could not understand what she said, but I knew that she was kind. I walked to a seat near the back of the room, where a girl smiled at me and spoke to me in a whisper that I also could not understand. What I remember most about that day, however, is that the morning was long, that I did not know where the bathroom was or how to ask if I could go, and that, frightened and miserable, I ran out of the room just a minute too late. I also remember the children laughing behind me as I ran.

Later on, when my sister comforted me gently as we waited for my mother to bring dry clothes from across the border, I hung my head in shame, much too embarrassed to look up. I wanted to tell the children who had laughed at me that English was the problem. But neither my sister nor I said anything to anyone.

In the years that I have spent studying Spanish–English bilingualism among Mexican-origin immigrants in the United States, I have spent many hours both in communities and in schools, and I have sought to understand how it is that individuals come to use two languages in their everyday lives. In many ways my own biography—the fact that I acquired English in a border area—has deeply influenced both the questions that I have asked about bilingualism and my own understanding of this phenomenon. There are themes—such as pain, embarrassment, and shame—that seem very important to me in understanding why different people learn or do not learn a second language.

Elisa, Bernardo, Lilian, and Manolo—the four young people I will describe in this book—enrolled in a middle school in a small community in the greater San Francisco Bay Area. They bravely began their struggle to learn English in order to acquire an education. All four of these children, however, were at risk. Immigrant students who enter American schools in the middle and high school years face a particularly difficult challenge. If they are to succeed in these schools, they must acquire English quickly. They must acquire enough English to participate in everyday social interactions with their peers and teachers, and they must acquire enough English to allow them to profit from subject-matter instruction conducted exclusively in this language. Newly arrived youngsters must acquire not only interpersonal communicative proficiency in English; they must also acquire academic proficiency. Interpersonal communicative proficiency involves the ability to speak and understand English in face-to-face interactions, while academic language proficiency involves, for example, the ability to comprehend extended spoken discourse on academic subjects, the ability to take notes when listening to such extended discourse, the ability to read extensively and intensively and to learn subject matter from such reading, and the ability to display what is learned in both oral and written modes.

Immigrant students entering American middle and high schools do not have much time. If they enter in the sixth grade, for example, they have only 6 years in which to develop age-appropriate abilities in English. Ironically, while they are developing such abilities in English, they may not be able to simultaneously develop their subject-matter knowledge. According to Berman and colleagues (1995) and Minicucci and Olsen (1992), enrollment in many classes—especially college-preparatory classes at the high school level—is open only to those students who have exited the ESL program and are considered to be "fully" proficient in English. Those students who do not reach this level—a level that is measured differently in different schools and school districts—will receive, at best, a limited education consisting of continuing ESL courses and a few subject-matter classes—designated ESL science, ESL social studies, or "sheltered" math—in which the subject matter normally studied in mainstream classes is covered only partially. Under the worst circumstances, these students will be enrolled exclusively in ESL, physical education, art, cooking, and other "undemanding" courses.

THE STUDY ITSELF

The study that I describe in this book took place over a 2-year period.[1] It involved a total of three middle schools, four Latino students who were studied in depth over that period, four different ESL teachers, and numerous subject-matter teachers who had the focal children in class. It also involved interviews with school personnel, with students themselves, and with their parents.

The study began in a single middle school that I have called here Garden Middle School. I received permission to work with one ESL teacher and to identify four newly arrived students whom I would shadow for a 2-year period. During the period of the study, I—together with Rosa Isela Rodríguez, then a doctoral student at the University of California–Berkeley—visited the school two to three times a week. During the second year, I also carried out observations at two other middle schools to which two of our focal students had transferred.

In general, we carried out observations at both schools by sitting in classrooms and tape-recording and/or taking notes of all activities and events observed. When allowed to do so, we walked around the room and interacted with small groups of students or otherwise participated in the activities in which students were engaged. We followed the four focal students to all their classes, focusing on a single student per visit.

The purpose of the observations we conducted in ESL classrooms was to collect information about the ESL instructional programs in which the students were enrolled. I wanted to see what students did in class as they studied English and how much access they had to English both in and outside of class. It was my intention to use the information gathered in classrooms as a background for the analysis of the focal students' English-language development in both oral and written modes.

Observations and tape-recordings of the subject-matter courses focused on the demands made by these classes on the oral and written English-language skills of both the focal students and other immigrant students in the school. Additionally, observations in the larger school context focused on peer relationships within the program and school, language use inside and outside of classrooms, sources of English inside and outside of classrooms, and the sources of written English surrounding students in the school setting.

During the 2-year period of the study, I also assessed students' productive and receptive skills in spoken and written English with specially designed procedures in order to record growth in speaking, listening, reading, and writing English. A total of four English-language proficiency assessments were made during the 2 years of the study. These assessments explored a range of both receptive and productive abilities and included a number of different tasks. While the exact nature of the tasks varied, depending on students and their willingness and ability to participate, students' performance in these simulated interactions offered important information about their developing proficiency in English over the 2-year period.

Because of the emphasis on writing development, I also collected written work produced by both the focal students and other students in the same classes, such as worksheets, written assignments, projects, tests, and other miscellaneous materials.

Additionally, in order to gain insights into the school's program for non-English-background students—its goals, design, and relative success—I interviewed the school principal, ESL teachers, teacher aides, subject-matter teachers, and other school personnel. The purpose of these interviews was to obtain information about: (1) levels of proficiency usually obtained by immigrant students in the course of 2 years, (2) general characteristics of "good" students, and (3) hypotheses about differences between and within groups.

Over the course of 2 years, I came to know Elisa, Lilian, Manolo, and Bernardo well. I saw Manolo and Bernardo make friends with other youngsters. I saw Elisa develop her first crush. I was there when Lilian was sent home for fighting. I saw them change from children to adolescents. Through it all, I also saw them struggle to speak and understand a new language. I learned about their parents and about their struggles in making sense of the world in which their children now lived.

Over the period of the study, I also came to know the school and the teachers well. Many spent long hours talking to me about their concerns. I met with both school and district administrators, attended community meetings on school issues, and slowly began to understand the politics of "White flight" in which the school district as well as its teachers and administrators were involved.

Today, a number of years after the study ended, much has happened in the lives of all four students. I have kept in close touch with both Lilian and Elisa, and I occasionally see Manolo and Bernardo. The schools in which I carried out the study continue to struggle to meet the needs of arriving immigrant students. What has become increasingly clear to me is that, in coming to this county and in adjusting to American schools, immigrant students and their families travel very long distances. These distances are physical, emotional, and psychological. And for many of these individuals, the journey from where they came from to becoming "American" will take a very long time indeed.

The dilemma facing schools is a difficult one. Students who arrive in this country *must* learn English. They cannot be truly accommodated by the schools until they can use English to achieve academically. At the same time, there is much confusion in educational circles and in the public mind about how students can best acquire the academic English skills required to succeed in school. It is my hope that this book, by offering a glimpse into the lives of four youngsters, may help to illustrate the kinds of struggles that learning English involves. Adequate policies and practices can only be implemented if policy makers, school administrators, and practitioners begin with a deep and clear understanding of the complexity of the issues surrounding the acquisition of English by minority youngsters.

1

Immigrant Children and the Teaching of English

In the last decade and a half, numerous countries around the world have grappled with questions surrounding the language to be used in the education of what have been termed linguistic-minority children. Publications focusing on language policies in education number in the hundreds and include examinations of language and education issues in Africa (Bokamba, 1991), India (Dua, 1991; Srivastava, 1988), the Philippines (Smolicz, 1986), Spain (Siguan, 1983), Australia (Kalantzis, Cope, & Slade, 1989), Germany (Raoufi, 1981), Belgium (Roosens, 1989), Jamaica (Craig, 1988), and Switzerland (Kolde, 1988). Additionally, a number of publications have examined specific aspects of education and language policies affecting linguistic minorities. Tosi (1989), for example, examined the entire issue of immigration and bilingual education in the European context. Churchill (1986) focused on the education of both indigenous and immigrant linguistic minorities. Spolsky (1986) focused on language barriers to education in multilingual settings, and Skutnabb-Kangas (1981) and Skutnabb-Kangas and Cummins (1988) examined minority education and community struggles for educational rights around the world. More recently, Glenn and de Jong (1996) have investigated policies and practices used to educate immigrant children in 12 different countries—Canada, Australia, Belgium, France, Germany, Sweden, the Netherlands, the United States, Switzerland, the United Kingdom, Denmark, and Norway.

In countries all over the world, children who do not speak the societal language face many difficulties in schools. It does not matter whether these youngsters are the children of indigenous minorities whose presence in a particular area of the world predates the formation of given nation-states or whether these youngsters are the children of newly arrived and often unwelcomed immigrants. Maori children in New Zealand, Lappish or Sami youngsters in Finland and Sweden, Turkish children in Germany, Algerian children in France, Pakistani children in England, and Mexican children in the United States all face similar difficulties at school: They do not speak the language spoken by their teachers at school.

The problem is not simple. As Churchill (1986) has pointed out, linguistic and cultural minorities have recently emerged as a central concern of educational policy in almost all member countries of the Organization for Economic Cooperation and Development (OECD).[1] What is evident from the examination of changing and shifting policies surrounding the education of immigrant children around the world is that policy development has often been the result of acrimonious national debates concerning the capacity of countries to assimilate very different people, the place of noncitizens and alien residents in a particular society, and the role of education in socializing new immigrants. In spite of important differences in specific circumstances, the questions surrounding the education of immigrant children are generally the same in many different parts of the world (Glenn & de Jong, 1996; Herriman, 1996; Lambert, 1994; Paulston, 1988; Thompson, Fleming, & Byram, 1996). Among these broad questions are the following:

1. What is the place of immigrants in the society?
2. What responsibilities does the nation have for educating the children of both legal and illegal immigrants?

Among the narrower questions focusing on educational policies and practices are the following:

1. In what ways is language a problem for children who arrive in schools without speaking the language of instruction?
2. For how long is language a problem for these children?
3. What specific difficulties do these children face in schools?
4. Are these difficulties primarily linguistic?
5. How similar are these difficulties to those experienced by majority-group children of similar socioeconomic backgrounds?
6. What languages should be used in educating immigrant children?
7. Should only the majority or societal language(s) be used?
8. If other languages are used, what criteria should determine which languages are selected?
9. If other languages are used, for how long should such languages be used?
10. If only the societal language is used, what kinds of language support do students need in order to achieve (as opposed to survive) in schools?

As will be noted, questions about appropriate or effective educational practices are necessarily embedded in larger questions concerning national identity and the responsibility of governments in educating immigrants.

In the United States, the same questions have surfaced in debates surrounding the education of the children of immigrants. Beginning during the time of increased immigration from southern and eastern Europe at the turn of the twentieth century, we have been concerned about these "new" Americans. In the early part of the century, for example, we worried about immigrants' ability to understand and embrace the principles of democracy. Language, however, did not move to the foreground as a central element but rather was seen as part of the process of Americanization (Bodnar, 1982; Dinnerstein, 1982; Fass, 1988; Handlin, 1951/1973, 1979, 1982; Olneck & Layerson, 1988; Perlmann, 1988; Spolsky,1986).

More recently, English itself has taken on greater importance in discussions surrounding the education of immigrant students. As Paulston (1986) has argued, at different points in time, groups in multiethnic societies can mobilize around symbols such as language or religion for particular purposes. Language can thus emerge as an important rallying point in boundary maintenance, as a way of defining "us" in comparison to "them." According to a number of scholars (e.g., Adams & Brink, 1990; Baron, 1990; Crawford, 1992; Daniels, 1990), efforts surrounding the establishment of English as the official language of the United States involve such a mobilization around language and reflect a concern—similar to that seen in Europe—about the ability of the United States to assimilate large numbers of very different groups of people.

Given this national climate, the teaching and learning of English have emerged as a central topic in conversations about the education of immigrant children. Indeed, the terms *teaching* and *learning* English are very much a part of our current national conversations surrounding the education of immigrant students. Newspaper reports (e.g., Asimov, 1998; Bazeley & Aratani, 1998), for example, often quote individuals who argue that children should quickly be "taught" English or who claim that they as young children "learned" English easily. What is not very clear is exactly what the public understands by the terms *to teach* and *to learn* English.

Part of the difficulty is that most policy makers and members of the public have little information about what actually happens in schools. In spite of that fact, however, far-reaching decisions are often made about immigrant children, about how they should be educated, and about which language should be used in their education. In the current context in which anti-immigrant sentiment is very strong, newly arrived children are routinely accused by the general public of not wanting to learn English and of failing to profit from the education that the state is giving them at great cost. Among policy makers and administrators, debates center around the English language and its place in educational institutions. There are many things, however, that these legislators do not know. They do not know, for example, that even when programs are conducted *entirely in English*, children have very little access to English. Because members of the public are not aware that in many schools English-language learners are segregated from their English-speaking peers, they imagine that in most schools non-English-speaking students have the opportunity of interacting with English speakers, of working collaboratively with such youngsters, or of hearing large amounts of English throughout the day. Policy makers do not know that the English newly arrived students hear often consists exclusively of bits and pieces of artificial-sounding language used in drills in their ESL classes or of the somewhat distorted language of subject-matter teachers who use "simplified" English in order to give students access to the curriculum.

THE NATIONAL CHALLENGE: EDUCATING ENGLISH-LANGUAGE LEARNERS

The nation's public schools now enroll a large number of students who have been identified as English-language learners (ELLs) by their local school districts. According to Macias and Kelly (1996), 3,184,696 (7.3%) English-language learners were enrolled in both public and nonpublic elementary school during the 1995–96 school year. The largest enrollments of ELL students were in California, Texas, New York, Florida, and Illinois. During the period of 1990–91 to 1994–95, 17 states reported increases in ELL enrollment of more than 10%. Seven states reported increases of more than 25%.[2]

According to *Prospects* (1995), Spanish was spoken by more than 77% of ELL children. Fifty-four percent of ELL students in first and third grades came from families with incomes of less than $15,000 and attended high-poverty schools. Nearly one out of four ELL students in classes with high concentrations of ELL students had repeated a grade by third grade as compared to 15 percent of other students. At the third-grade level, ELL students scored at the 30th percentile in reading and 36th percentile in math.

Even though a number of weaknesses have been identified in the collection and reporting of education statistics for ELL students (e.g., August & Hakuta, 1997; Hopstock & Bucaro, 1993), a sense of the challenges facing American schools can been seen from work carried out by a number of researchers (e.g., Bradby, 1992; Fleischman & Hopstock, 1993; McArthur,

1993; Moss & Puma, 1995). In 1992, for example, 42 percent of persons aged 16 to 24 who reported difficulty with English had dropped out of high school (McArthur, 1993).

The challenges of educating students who do not speak a societal language are enormous. In the United States, it is not just a question of teaching English; rather, it is a question of providing large numbers of students with access to the curriculum at the same time that they are learning English. Key sources of federal law (Title VI of the Civil Rights Act of 1964, *Lau v. Nichols*, the Equal Educational Opportunities Act of 1974, *Castañeda v. Pickard*) prohibit discrimination against students on the basis of language and require that districts take affirmative steps to overcome language barriers. *Castañeda v. Pickard*, in particular, makes clear that districts have a dual obligation to teach English and to provide access to academic-content instruction. Programs designed for English-language learners, in theory, must ensure that students either "keep up" with age-appropriate academic content while they are learning English or, if they are instructed exclusively in English as a second language for a period of time, that they are given the means to "catch up" with the academic content covered by their same-age peers. It is especially important that, in either case, ELL learners do not incur irreparable deficits in subject-matter learning.

As shown in Figure 1.1, there are four different instructional options available for elementary school children who have limited proficiency in English: English-only, English-only with ESL, and two types of bilingual education programs. The most common option (English-only programs) is referred to as either *immersion* by its supporters or *submersion* by its critics. In such programs, ELL students are placed in totally English instruction along with their mainstream peers. In many schools, such placement is complemented with pull-out programs in English as a second language. ELL children are removed or pulled out from their regular classroom and join other students for possibly an hour's direct instruction in English. Very few teachers are able to provide students with the opportunity to make up missed classroom instruction.

Bilingual education, while much discussed around the country, is an option actually open to only a small fraction of ELL children, primarily in the first 3 years of schooling. In California, for example, before the passage of Proposition 227 (which abolished bilingual education in the state[3]), only 409,874 children of a total of 1,406,166 English-language learners were enrolled in bilingual education programs (Rumberger, 1998). Similarly, in other parts of the country, bilingual education programs, when they exist, are mainly transitional. They move children quickly into English-only education.

Figure 1.1. Language learning and academic-subject instruction options in elementary schools

Program Type	Definition	Classroom Population	Comments
English-only	All subject matter taught in English	Anglophone and ELL children	No support provided for ELL students
English-only with ESL	English with English-as-a-second-language (ESL) instruction with special teacher	Anglophone and ELL children	ELL children taken from classroom for special instruction
Bilingual education (transitional)	Minority language used to teach concepts; English used increasingly	ELL children	Primarily implemented in grades K–3; children transferred to all-English programs after grade 3
Bilingual education (maintenance)	Minority language *and* English used to teach concepts after English is acquired	ELL children	Focus on continued development of both English and the minority language; very few such programs beyond grade 3

The challenges for schools and teachers are even greater at the middle school and high school levels. As shown in Figure 1.2, enrollment options for ELL students are different at the middle school and high school levels. At these levels, instruction in a student's primary language is exceedingly rare. Some school districts place students in intensive ESL instruction (called "newcomer programs") for a semester or a year and then place them in two or three periods of ESL instruction and a set of other courses called "ESL subject matter" or "sheltered courses."

For schools, the presence of large numbers of newly arrived immigrant students means that they must find ways of educating such students while still educating mainstream students as well. They must find regular teachers willing to work with such students or hire specially trained teachers to teach them. They must establish ESL programs, newcomer programs, sheltered programs, and other kinds of support mechanisms that will help students learn both English and subject-matter content.

Some schools are more successful than others. Some have fewer numbers of immigrant students or greater numbers of trained teachers. Others

Figure 1.2. Language learning and academic-subject instruction options in the
secondary schools

Program Type	Definition	Classroom Population	Comments
Newcomer programs	Self-contained intensive ESL	ELL students who are newly arrived	Students focus exclusively on English for a specific period of time.
ESL instruction	Instruction in English as a second language; focus primarily on grammar and lexis	ELL students	Students may spend up to three periods a day in ESL classes.
Sheltered Instruction Subject-matter instruction for ELL students	Specially designed instruction in English in regular subjects; math, social studies, science, etc., intended for ELL students and delivered using simplified/planned language	ELL students	Students spend several periods a day in ESL instruction and also enroll in special subject matter courses designed for ELL students. There is limited coverage of the regular curriculum.
English-only	Regular classes	Anglophone and ELL students	No special support provided for ELL students

face many challenges and find few easy answers. At some schools, immigrant students arrive at the middle school and high school levels having
never attended school in their home countries. Along with them arrive
other students eager to learn and excited about the opportunity to study in
this country.

Newly arrived immigrant Latino students who enter American schools
at the middle school and secondary levels face particularly difficult challenges (Chamot, 1992; Davis & McDaid, 1992; LaFontaine, 1987; Lucas,
1992; Minicucci & Olsen, 1992; Portes & Gran; 1991; Rumbaut, 1990).
There is much that teachers do not know about how the English language
develops in second-language learners, and there is little information available to guide them in determining when ESL students at different levels can
"compete" with mainstream students. Many of them, therefore, elect to
have very little to do with students who speak and write very "imperfect"
English.

Given such responses by teachers, in many schools there are currently two separate worlds: the world of ESL and the mainstream world in which real American schooling takes place (Harklau, 1994a, 1994b, 1994c, 1999). ESL students become locked into a holding pattern in which they enroll in sequences of more and more ESL courses and in "accessible" subjects such as art, cooking, and physical education. All too often, students who enter school in the middle school years become what some practitioners have referred to as ESL "lifers."[4] They will remain in ESL for the rest of their academic lives. They enter middle school as part of the ESL track and remain in this same separate world during their entire 4 years of high school as well. In the best of cases, even when they are "mainstreamed" in other subject-matter classes, few non-English-background students ever manage to enroll in *regular* (non-ESL) college-prep English courses. With rare exceptions, mainstream English teachers find it impossible to teach English and American literature to students whose English is still flawed. They argue, for example, that they cannot accept writing on literary topics that still contains many "mechanical" errors not typical of native English-speaking students.

Unfortunately, given the increasing numbers of non-English-speaking students, it is estimated (August & Hakuta, 1997; Chamot, 1992; Davis & McDaid, 1992; Garcia, in press; LaFontaine, 1987; Lucas, 1992; Minicucci & Olsen, 1992; Portes & Gran, 1991; Rumbaut, 1990) that two-thirds of limited-English-speaking children are not receiving the language assistance they need in order to succeed in their academic and intellectual development. The lack of support services is especially evident at the secondary level. The result of this is that talented students are often lost to the world of education. Whatever interest and love they might have had for subjects they had studied before they arrived here must be put on an indefinite hold. The possibility of continuing to grow intellectually must be deferred until such time as they are considered to be able to "handle" English.

It is very easy to place blame. The truth is, however, that any assignment of blame must take into consideration the fact that there is little consensus on how much English is enough English to allow such students to participate meaningfully in courses taught in English. Common sense would suggest that an ability to follow English explanations and to understand English-language texts might be sufficient to allow students to enroll in such courses. Indeed, experience with foreign students in American universities—before the development of formalized ESL programs—would suggest that it is possible for students to profit from instruction in English, that is, to learn through English even when their productive skills (speaking and writing) have not developed fully.

The dilemma for American educators, however, involves not just determining whether students can learn from instruction given in English. In order to make good decisions about how best to educate English-language learners, school personnel must also be concerned about teacher expectations, classroom traditions, new standards, and statewide achievement testing in a political climate that has become increasingly hostile to immigrants. In California and in many other parts of the country, the controversies surrounding the education of immigrant students are serious and far-reaching. They continue to be part of a political debate that one can only expect will grow more bitter. Supporters of Proposition 227, for example, are currently attempting to persuade voters in other states that the problem surrounding the low achievement of immigrant children is simply the existence of bilingual education. They do not talk about the complexity of the issues. They do not mention that the majority of California ELL children had no support for learning English or for keeping up with their same-age peers. They will not admit that there are no easy solutions to the problem and that *with* or *without* bilingual education, the challenges remain.

THE ACQUISITION OF ENGLISH IN CLASSROOM SETTINGS

Currently, many policy makers and members of the public—even those who have been relatively unsuccessful as classroom language learners—have expressed very strong opinions about the teaching of English to immigrant students. Many believe, for example, that language study is very much like the study of other subjects and that language can be "taught" and "learned" in a short period of time. Many attribute the difficulties in learning English experienced by youngsters in school to their community's lack of commitment to becoming American. Others have strongly argued that the availability of primary-language instruction (i.e., bilingual education) prevents children from having to push themselves to learn English.

Unfortunately, the process of acquiring a second language is much more complex than these opinions suggest. In the following sections, I offer a brief overview of what we know about second-language acquisition from the research perspective. I contrast that perspective with that of second-language teachers who are engaged in the teaching of English in real classrooms. Finally, I describe the kinds of language proficiencies that must be developed by ELL students in order to succeed in school as well as the challenges that these youngsters face in acquiring such proficiencies in second-language classrooms.

Research in Second-Language Acquisition

The field of second-language acquisition (SLA) is a relatively new field of inquiry that takes theories and methodologies from a number of disciplines (psycholinguistics, sociolinguistics, social psychology, and neurolinguistics) and uses them to understand the process of second- and foreign-language acquisition in instructional and noninstructional settings. Since the mid-1960s, SLA researchers have given much attention to the characteristics of the language produced by learners, to the linguistic environment necessary for second-language (L2) acquisition, to individual differences in second-language learning, and to the process of L2 acquisition in naturalistic and instructional settings. In spite of the attention given to these issues, recent reviews of the literature (August & Hakuta, 1997; Bialystok & Hakuta, 1994; Ellis, 1990; Larsen-Freeman & Long, 1991; Pica, 1994; Skehan, 1989; Spolsky, 1989) point out that there is much that we do not currently know about the process of second-language acquisition.

Most researchers, however, agree that the acquisition of L2 proficiency, which is not identical to the acquisition of a first language (L1), involves an active construction on the part of the learner. In naturalistic settings, learners internalize a knowledge of the L2 through observation and participation in communication. The process of L2 acquisition is not linear. Learners do not begin with "simple" structures and proceed to "complex" ones. Instead, they attempt to communicate and, in so doing, they incorporate elements of the first and the second languages as well as elements that are not a part of L1 or L2 to create a series of overlapping approximative systems (Nemser, 1971) or interlanguages (Selinker, 1972, 1992). These interlanguages or approximative systems have their own distinct grammar, are systematic and rule-governed, and are common to all learners. Moreover, regardless of the first-language background of learners, interlanguages exhibit a common accuracy/acquisition order (Larson-Freeman & Long, 1991). In English, for example, L2 learners acquire morphemes (e.g., those indicating the past tense, plural, and possessive) in the same order as do children acquiring English as an L1 (Johnston, 1985). Interlanguages, then, exhibit a common developmental sequence that is similar to that of L1-speaking children (Ravem, 1968, 1974). For example, L2 learners, in acquiring English *Wh-* questions, move through the same sequence of stages as do children learning English as a first language. This is true for English-language learners from many different language backgrounds (Meisel, Clahsen, & Pienemann, 1981). Contrary to the strong version of the contrastive analysis hypothesis, which assumed that all L2 errors could be predicted by comparing the differences between the first language and the target language, systematic error analysis of language produced by L2 learners has revealed that the first language is not the only or even primary source of errors encountered in the interlanguages of second-language learners (Faerch & Kasper, 1987; Gass, 1984).

Unlike the learning of a first language, which is accomplished successfully by all normal human beings, research on SLA reveals that there are many individual differences in the learning of a second language. For reasons that researchers do not entirely understand, many, if not most, second-language learners do not completely acquire nativelike proficiency in a second language. This is true for learners who attempt to study a second language primarily in a classroom setting as well as for learners who use a second language in their daily lives for many years. Research focusing on differences in attainment among learners has focused on such factors as age of acquisition, language aptitude, motivation, personality, and cognitive style.

As opposed to what is generally believed by the public about the natural superiority of children as L2 learners, there are many disagreements among researchers about age and L2 acquisition. Most researchers (e.g., Bialystok & Hakuta, 1994; Larsen-Freeman & Long, 1991), in reviewing existing research, conclude that older means faster in terms of rate of acquisition of morphology and syntax, while younger is better in terms of final level of attainment of accent-free, nativelike proficiency. They also point out, however, that explanations for differences in attainment (including social and experiential factors as well as biological explanations such as the critical period hypothesis or the sensitive period hypothesis) are limited in explanatory power. Some researchers (e.g., Ekstrand, 1981) conclude that there is no evidence for a biologically determined optimal age for L2 acquisition. Ekstrand argues that children do not have a greater facility for learning language. They are simply engaged in a less complex task for which they have more time. Other researchers (e.g., Bialystok & Hakuta, 1994) concur and point out that the only convincing evidence of differences between children and adults is in the area of phonology. In all other areas, the *process* of L2 acquisition is similar for both adults and children. An adult learning a second language behaves just like a child acquiring a second language. The differences in their ultimate attainment, therefore, need not be explained by a biological critical or sensitive period.

The Classroom Context

A number of researchers have sought to examine the kind of environment/interactions/conditions that must be present in classroom settings in order for language acquisition to take place. The assumption underlying such research, as Ellis (1992) pointed out, is that L2 acquisition will be most successful in those classrooms in which conditions are similar to those found in naturalistic environments.

Some researchers have focused on the characteristics of the input available to learners in the classroom. Krashen (1985), for example, maintains that learners require access to comprehensible input, that is, to language—made comprehensible in a variety of ways by the instructor—that is a step beyond their levels of acquisition. According to Krashen, if the input is sufficient, the necessary grammar is automatically provided and the learner proceeds through a natural process of acquisition. For Krashen, the classroom is important because it offers the learner access to meaningful language. From this meaningful classroom language, the learner builds an approximative system that can subsequently be used in interactions with real speakers in order to acquire other elements of the L2. There are many questions, however, about what comprehensible input is and about the ways in which teachers should modify their language. Some researchers (Kleifgen, 1985; Wong Fillmore, 1985) suggest that, ideally, input is adjusted by teachers according to feedback provided by learners.

Long (1983), while agreeing that input is important, argues that acquisition results not from comprehension but from interaction. He maintains (Long, 1981, 1983) that negotiation involving two-way communication is essential. Swain (1985), on the other hand, contends that production, not comprehension, may move the learner to attend to and therefore to acquire grammatical proficiency in a language. Comprehensible output (the production of language that is comprehensible to native-speaker interlocutors) allows learners to test hypotheses about the language system and to move to more grammatically accurate output. Ellis (1988), however, after reviewing numerous studies on the relationship between learner participation and L2 acquisition, concludes that results are mixed. It is not clear whether participation causes acquisition or whether acquisition causes participation. For some students, performing in the classroom leads to high anxiety.

In carrying out research in classrooms, some researchers have paid particular attention to the effect of form-focused language instruction on rate and level of L2 acquisition, on the process of L2 acquisition, on the order and sequence of acquisition, and on accuracy. Some researchers (e.g., Lightbown, 1983, 1984) view explicit grammar instruction as direct interference with the learning process and have strongly questioned the restriction of learners to a limited diet of structure-by-structure teaching. They view classroom activities devoted exclusively to practice with unrelated sentences as contexts in which learners will not be exposed to adequate input.

Findings from research on formal language instruction are mixed, and many studies fail to describe the exact nature of the formal instruction involved as well as the precise characteristics of classroom interaction. However, Ellis (1990) concludes that, although there is some evidence that formal language instruction can support more rapid and higher levels of acquisition, this evidence must be interpreted with caution. In general, according to Ellis, the research evidence suggests that form-focused instruction does not (1) prevent developmental errors, (2) change the order of acquisition of morphemes or syntactical features, (3) result in greater accuracy in spontaneous utterances, or (4) enable learners to acquire developmental features out of order. Pienemann (1985) argues that formal instruction will only promote the acquisition of a structure if the interlanguage is at a stage where that structure would soon be acquired in the natural setting. Very few features are teachable at any one time, and the effects of instruction on the acquisition of those features may be temporary. Some scholars see interlanguages as highly resistant to modification by direct form-focused instruction. Moreover, they maintain that little is known about the delayed effects of such instruction. Other researchers (e.g., Lightbown, 1992) disagree, arguing that focus on form can be effective at the moment that learners attempt to communicate specific ideas. A few students of SLA (e.g., Long & Robinson, 1998) argue for the benefits of inducing learners to attend to form in meaningful contexts as they arise incidentally in lessons. Doughty (1998), while admitting that there is little evidence supporting form-focused instruction during meaningful communication, is optimistic that its integration into communicative language teaching will result in a more efficient process of L2 acquisition.

Second-Language Teaching

In spite of the questions and concerns that second-language researchers have about L2 instruction and its effect on acquisition, many, if not most, second-language teachers assume that language elements can be taught in order and that students who are diligent and studious will be able to learn them. Second-language teachers see themselves as engaged in the process of teaching an *academic subject*. They impart instruction, they assign work, they assess student learning, and they grade students on their academic achievement. Unfortunately, classroom success is often based on elements such as homework completion, project completion, and test grades. Final grades in a particular second-language course may not be related to the development of proficiency in the target language.

   In their institutions, second-language teachers are members of language-teaching departments in which a set of sequential courses dictates many of the objectives of their instruction. The practices and approaches that they use in the classroom are influenced primarily by trends and traditions of instruction within the discipline of second-language teaching, by their own experiences as language learners, and by the expectations of the particular institution in which they are teaching. Classroom practices are also deeply influenced by curricular documents and state frameworks as well as by available classroom materials and assessment procedures used to measure student progress.

Methods in Second-Language Teaching

In carrying out their work, most second-language teachers see themselves as using practices and procedures that are recognized as effective teaching methods. Unfortunately, as Richards and Rodgers (1986) point out, the field of second-language teaching has been characterized by a proliferation of both approaches (philosophies of language at the level of theory and principles) and methods (procedures for teaching language). In many cases, widely heralded "new" methods turn out to be variations on old approaches. In other cases, new methods are an attempt to combine classroom practices that are based on various different approaches to both language and language learning. In a few cases, new methods (e.g., the natural approach [Terrell, 1977]) reflect an attempt to build on current thinking in second-language acquisition. Such methods often involve a total departure from time-honored practices in the profession and are rarely adopted entirely by most teachers. Even those who support a particular innovation often argue for *informed eclecticism,* a view holding that teachers can selectively bring together a combination of best practices without concern about underlying theories of language and language learning. The difficulty of combining methods can perhaps be appreciated in the following summaries of several widely used second-language teaching methods and their underlying theories.

The grammar-translation method, for example, was initially used in the teaching of Latin. Still used today, it organizes instruction around a syllabus that includes rules and facts of language, use of unrelated sentences for translation practice, translation of literary texts, the study of vocabulary needed for text translation, and deductively taught grammar. The students' L1 is the medium of instruction, and students are expected to study and learn rules. The teacher is expected to present rules and correct errors.

The audiolingual method, used extensively some 15 to 20 years ago, views language as a set of structures that can be described at different levels (phonemic, morphemic, syntactic, etc.). Focusing primarily on oral language, its theory of language learning is behaviorist. Stimulus, response, and reinforcement are important. The syllabus is organized around key phonological, morphological, and syntactic elements. Contrastive analysis is used for selection of elements, and grammar is taught inductively. Dialogues and drills are used extensively as students respond to stimuli, memorize, repeat, and imitate. Teachers are seen as models of language who conduct drills, teach dialogues, and direct choral response.

The communicative method, variarions of which are currently used, views language as communication and sees the goal of language study as acquiring communicative competence. It assumes that activities involving communication and meaningful tasks promote learning. Syllabi for communicative courses vary but generally include structures and functions and task-based activities. Students are expected to play the role of negotiators, contributors, and actors. Teachers are expected to facilitate the communication process, to participate in communication, and to analyze the communicative needs of students.

The natural approach, by comparison, views language as a vehicle for communicating meanings and messages. Its theory of language learning, based on the work of Krashen (1985), includes the acquisition/learning hypothesis, the monitor hypothesis, the natural order hypothesis, the input hypothesis, and the affective filter hypothesis. Classroom activities are organized around the processing of comprehensible input. Students are expected to move through a series of stages in developing oral proficiency, including the preproduction stage, the early production stage, and the speech emergent stage. Teachers are expected to provide input and to create a supportive classroom environment. Teachers of sheltered classes for ELL students often claim to be using the natural approach.

Underlying each of these methods are very clear positions on language itself, the ways in which languages are learned, and the kinds of classroom activities that can best bring about learning. In many cases, theories about language and language acquisition underlying one method directly contradict those underlying others. Audiolingualism, for example, which views language as a habit-learning process, is incompatible with the natural method, in which the acquisition of structures is considered to depend on language that is understood.

It should be noted that existing methods have focused primarily on oral language. Classroom procedures and practices are generally more developed for working with the spoken language than they are for developing academic language proficiencies in learners.

When teachers describe themselves as eclectic and report, for example, combining grammar-translation with communicative language teaching, it is very possible that they are not fully aware of the contradictory positions of the two approaches. On the other hand, it may be the case that teachers are less concerned about the incompatibility of underlying theories than they are about students' passing required examinations. They may be aware, for example, that, although members of their department speak eloquently about the importance of communicative skills, they continue to give tests on key grammatical points and structures. In spite of their own positions on L2-acquisition theory, teachers may see themselves as obligated to prepare their students for the required assessments. They may, therefore, combine methods they know to be fundamentally incompatible.

Materials Used in Second-Language Teaching

For most teachers, regardless of their theoretical or methodological orientation, the textbook has the most direct immediate influence on their teaching. For young teachers, it is often the textbook that serves as a syllabus for the course and that defines the types of activities that will take place in the classroom.

In the case of the language-teaching field, textbooks and ancillary materials—while often giving lip service to research on second-language acquisition or to current thinking in the profession about language teaching—tend to be conservative in orientation. The presentation of language structures is traditional and often similar to that found in audiolingual textbooks or even textbooks based on grammar-translation. Grammar makes up the core of the material to be covered. In many recent textbooks, however, presentations on structure are complemented by pair- and group-discussion activities, communicatively oriented practice of vocabulary and structures, and reading and writing activities. Some textbooks also include listening tasks based on the covered structures, vocabulary, or thematic units.

There are many differences, however, between textbooks used in the teaching of foreign languages and those used in the teaching of English as a second language in this country. These differences reveal a great deal about the ways in which instruction is envisioned for mainstream students who study foreign languages as elective subjects and for newly arrived immigrant students who undertake the study of English in order to succeed in school. Foreign-language textbooks (e.g., Spanish, German, French) produced for the middle school level are normally at least 2 inches thick and contain colorful illustrations of interactions containing phrases students are expected to learn, vocabulary lists, grammatical explanations, fun-filled related activities, readings, and supported writing assignments. A large number of ancillary materials are provided by the publishers, including overhead transparencies, audiotapes, and computer disks. Importantly, *both English and the target language* are used as languages of instruction. At the beginning of most textbooks, explanations for reading the text, for completing exercises, for reading cultural materials, and for developing language-learning strategies are given *in English*. In later chapters, a transition is made to an increasing use of the target language in the same sections. All materials contain a full English glossary that students use to look up unknown words. Many readings are annotated in English with key cultural information asking students to note particular differences or similarities. Developers of foreign-language materials are required by state adoption policies, and therefore by their publishers, to view students as competent speakers of English who can use their L1 to understand how the target language works and to provide them with access to meaning. Textbooks are designed so that students are not entirely dependent on the teacher.

As compared to texts used in middle schools for studying foreign languages, text materials in ESL tend to be published as sets of related texts. Instead of a single textbook organized around themes and focusing on all four skills (i.e., speaking, listening, reading, and writing) as an integrated whole, publishers often produce a set of related course texts, each of which focuses on a different objective (e.g., listening, writing). It is frequently the case that school districts buy only the texts focusing on a particular objective (e.g., spoken language, reading) and assume that teachers will complement these materials with their own.

It is especially important to note that all text materials sold in this country for ESL instruction are written exclusively in English. There are no handy glossaries in the students' native language and no annotations of readings. Students cannot look up unknown words quickly when working on exercises. Moreover, because vocabulary lists often depend on ambiguous drawings, youngsters often reach wrong conclusions about word meanings. It is possible, for example, for students to assume that the English word *hat*, illustrated by a picture of a man with a hat, means "man" rather than "hat."

Most ESL instructors maintain a strict English-only policy in their classrooms and speak entirely in English to their students, even when they have homogeneous classes and are fluent in other languages.[5] As a result, beginning students may struggle to make sense of the expressions and vocabulary they are expected to learn. They may simply repeat after their teachers and fill in workbook exercises without understanding the expressions or structures they are practicing. Even when they are able to understand the meanings of some words or structures, they must take extensive notes in order to be able to study outside of class unless they are allowed to write in their textbooks.

Unlike foreign-language textbooks, ESL textbooks have no text segments in students' native languages dedicated to teaching students strategies for learning vocabulary, for guessing words in context, or for developing listening comprehension. As a result, students are entirely dependent on the teacher and on fellow students who may know a little more English than they do.

ELL Students in Schools

For non-English-background students whose future depends on acquiring English, how well the language is "taught" and how successful schools are in creating a context in which students have access to English during the schoolday will determine to a very large extent how quickly and how well these youngsters acquire English.

Over the course of the last 15 years, a number of researchers have examined the language demands of all-English classrooms and the effect of particular language-teaching practices on academic achievement. From Wong Fillmore (1982), for example, we learn that in order to participate in the life and work of schools and in order to learn academic subject matter, immigrant students must develop two fundamental skills in English: (1) They must be able to comprehend the spoken language of their teachers as they explain and present instruction, and (2) they must comprehend the language of textbooks from which they are expected to learn.

The current *ESL Standards for Pre-K–12 Students* (TESOL, 1997) directly address the confusion surrounding the goals of English-language study by delineating progress indicators of English-language development for ESL teachers and administrators. These standards specify the language skills English-language learners need in order to have "unrestricted access to grade-appropriate instruction in challenging academic subjects" (TESOL, 1997, pp. 1–2) and stress that learners need to develop English proficiency in order to participate in social interactions as well as to achieve academically in all content areas. Specifically, the three goals of English-language learning involve (1) using English to communicate in social settings, (2) using English to achieve academically in all content areas, and (3) using English in socially and culturally appropriate ways. The standards stress that English-language learners must develop abilities to request and provide information, to paraphrase a teacher's directions, to work successfully with partners, to negotiate and reach consensus, to compare and contrast information, to read and get meaning from texts, to gather evidence, to prepare and participate in debates, and to edit and revise written assignments. They must, moreover, be able to choose the language variety (e.g., standard American English, Chicano English, Puerto Rican English), the register (i.e., level of language), and the genre (rhetorical mode) that is appropriate to the interaction, interlocutor, and setting. They must respond to humor, express anger, make polite requests, carry on small talk, and recognize and use idiomatic speech.

The most important goal of ESL study in schools today is the development of proficient academic English. In order to develop such competence, students must learn how individuals use language effectively to achieve different purposes, how discourse conventions work (how texts, both oral and written, are structured), and how the language system operates. They must use all of this knowledge *together* in the process of transmitting and receiving meaningful messages and especially in continuing to learn through the medium of English.

According to Wong Fillmore (1991), the necessary ingredients for second-language learning include:

> (1) learners who realize that they need to learn the target language (TL) and are motivated to do so; (2) speakers of the target language who know it well enough to provide the learners with access to the language and the help for learning it; and (3) a social setting which brings learners and TL speakers into frequent enough contact to make language learning possible. (p. 52)

Unfortunately, as the following chapters make clear, these three ingredients are rarely present in the lives of immigrant youngsters. As Garcia (in press) has pointed out, newly arrived students are isolated in their communities, in their neighborhoods, and in their schools and classrooms. Learning academic English does not take place rapidly.

In the chapters that follow, I portray the community and the school in which this study took place and examine the isolation of newly arrived children in ESL classrooms. I then describe the second-language-teaching program at the school and the ways in which teachers were influenced by local conditions as well as by the traditions in language teaching that I have described above.

In Chapters 4 through 7, I present extended descriptions of the four focal students: Lilian, Elisa, Manolo, and Bernardo. I describe their behavior in the classroom, the strategies they evolved to survive in the school setting, and the progress they made in acquiring English. Finally, in Chapter 8, I examine the experiences of the four youngsters, analyze their success or lack of success in learning English, and examine the implications of their experiences for both policy and practice.

The Town, the School, and the Students

At 11:00 in the morning, Victor Andrade is still hopeful. After riding his bicycle for almost an hour, he has been standing at the intersection of Hacienda Avenue and San Martin Road in Mission Vista since 6:00. He knows that if he is lucky, he will be hired to do a day's work in construction, or gardening, or painting. Victor isn't picky. Like the other Latino men standing on the corner, he hopes for a day's wages, maybe $50 for 8 hours of hard work.

Many area residents know about the men standing on the corner because they are a source of enthusiastic cheap labor. Contractors, landscapers, and plumbers often come by early in the morning and hire a dozen men. Other area residents who just need one or two men for hauling, digging, and loading come by the intersection later.

At 11:30, a pickup truck pulls up and a man puts out his hand. "*Cuatro*," he shouts in Spanish, holding up four fingers, as the waiting men run toward the truck. Six or seven men climb aboard, but the man is firm. "*Cuatro*," he insists, "*cuatro*." Three men jump out of the truck. Victor is one of them. This time, he wasn't fast enough. He walks slowly back to the corner and joins the ten or fifteen men who still wait. He is tired and he is hungry.

Victor is one of many men who gather every day on one corner in a small shopping center in the city of Mission Vista. They are *jornaleros*, men who do a day's work for a stated wage. They stand on the corner much like they did in Mexico, where the contracting of jornaleros on the street is a normal occurrence. The men want work, and they have no other way of contacting potential employers. By standing on the corner and eagerly running toward every car that slows down, the men want to impress potential employers with their eagerness and enthusiasm. They are hard workers. They will spend hours in the sun, in the rain, and in the cold.

They chop wood, dig trenches, dig up tree stumps, clean warehouses. They are not proud. Work is work, and they need money for their families.

Businessowners in the small shopping center, however, are angry and complain that their clients are frightened away by the presence of the Mexican workers. Some claim that their customers are pestered; others claim that the men are dirty and unsightly; still others claim that they are intimidated by what they suspect to be illegal aliens in their community.

In the surrounding community, feelings about immigrant day workers run high. Area residents have protested the presence of Mexican workers on their street corners. One town has passed an antiloitering ordinance forbidding several people from congregating on street corners. Another town has passed a law banning solicitation of work from vehicles.

In the community where this study took place, defenders of the day laborers attempted to appease businessowners and angry residents by raising money for a workers' center. They claimed that such a center would remove workers from in front of businesses and still provide them with the opportunity of finding work. They also argued that a center would protect laborers from unscrupulous contractors who ordinarily hired them for very low wages.

Citizens angry about the workers' presence in their community, in turn, claimed that most men were illegal aliens, led unstable lives, and, because they spoke no English, had little opportunity for other jobs. They accused workers of loitering, littering, drinking, urinating in public, and intimidating women. According to one newspaper story, members of one activist group, which strongly opposed the job center proposal, photographed workers and wrote down license plate numbers of employers as a way of pressuring "illegal" workers to get off the streets. They then pressed immigration officials to conduct raids.

Elisa, Lilian, Bernardo, and Manolo, the focal children in this study, all lived and went to school in the town that I call Mission Vista. They felt the tensions present in the community through their parents, their relatives, and their friends. While it is not clear that they understood what these tensions meant, every day they walked to the middle-class part of town to attend a school that until a few years before had been almost exclusively White. They saw other students arrive in Mercedes-Benzes and BMWs, delivered lovingly at school by well-dressed and confident parents. Immigrant children, on the other hand, walked to school, no matter where they lived. School bus service had been discontinued in the district as a cost-cutting measure.

What happened in the community among both majority and minority residents, what happened in government agencies and religious institutions, and what was reported by the mass media were directly related to what happened to the four children in school. As Cortes (1986) has suggested, in order to understand a school context, the wider context in which a school is located must be examined carefully. What happens in the school-yard, in attendance offices, in PTA meetings, and at school board meetings directly reflects the beliefs and values of the community and its residents. In the case of communities such as Mission Vista where rapid population shift had resulted in a changing community, established middle-class residents necessarily come into contact with people who are very different from themselves. Often established residents struggle to retain control of the schools. At other times, they simply give up and decide to send their children to private schools. They abandon institutions that they had helped support and maintain for many years.

The process of confronting and adjusting to change is a painful one. In the face of rapid population shift, the entire character of both the community and the schools change. "New" children are unlike the "old" children. Expectations that teachers have about study habits, background knowledge, language, and discipline are found to be inaccurate. Assumptions about children's futures must be questioned. Views about curriculum and standards, as well as opportunities to learn, cannot be taken for granted. Some teachers feel angry. They feel cheated at not having the "good" students they once had. They join together to complain to the principal. The solution, they argue, is to hire more new teachers to handle students who are not up to their standards. Principals, however, do not have easy solutions. Sometimes they, too, wish that the new children would simply go away.

NEW IMMIGRANTS IN MISSION VISTA

Mission Vista is located in California. It is home to numerous high-technology companies as well as retail stores, executive offices, research and development firms, and professional service companies. The brochures mailed out by the Chamber of Commerce depict an attractive community blessed with a desirable climate, a good transportation network, and two nearby international airports. At the time that the study took place, the average price of a single family home was $394,971. A studio or one-bedroom apartment rented for $600 to $850. Apartments with two to four bedrooms rented for $800 to $2,100. Residences—including apartments and single-family homes—in the community were 35.5% owner-occupied and 64.5% renter-occupied.

Beginning in late 1980s, Mission Vista schools experienced a rapid population change. Large numbers of Latino immigrants of largely Mexican background moved into the community primarily because of the availability of apartment rentals. The arrival of Mexican immigrants from a largely rural background was felt in many ways by the community. Large sections of the town suddenly took on a different character. Apartment buildings that were built as luxury rentals 20 or 30 years earlier became the heart of the immigrant community. Blocks and blocks of two-story apartment complexes were slowly neglected by their owners. Swimming pools were emptied or boarded over. Buildings were not repainted. Two or three families often occupied two-bedroom apartments, and dozens of young children played in the dirt and mud surrounding the run-down buildings. Old cars lined the streets, and mothers pushing strollers—with three or four young children in tow—could be seeing walking many blocks to the grocery store. On weekends, very large extended families invaded the city parks and took over the picnic grounds and the grassy areas for noisy games of soccer. Hamburger franchises and supermarket chains found themselves competing with hole-in-the-wall Mexican restaurants and tiny grocery stores. Permanent residents were not prepared for the changes when they happened. What had once been a largely middle-class community saw itself slowly sliding into an identity that it did not want. Very few things appeared to be sacred. Even the area soccer leagues were threatened. Through the school, immigrant parents requested that their children be allowed to play. Middle-class soccer parents in Mission Vista, however, were not ready to mingle with immigrant parents. They lobbied the community youth sports association to insist on the customary $50-dollar-per-child fee. When the school raised money to pay the required fees, separate teams were organized for Latino children.

Much attention in the community was also directed at "gang" activity. A gang was defined as an association of youngsters who dressed alike and spent time together in groups. It was assumed in both the community and the school that gang membership was a problem for Latino students in particular. While it is not clear that all youngsters who dressed in certain colors or drew particular symbols on their notebooks were affiliated with gangs, the Mission Vista police department organized itself to inform schools about gang "wannabe" activities that needed to be monitored. Reflecting in part the rising anti-immigrant sentiment in California and in part the changes that surrounded them, residents of Mission Vista engaged in a not-so-subtle campaign to keep their communities "safe," their parks clean, and their schools organized primarily to serve the needs of their own children.

Many battles were fought at school board meetings. School administrators fought to implement new programs that could serve immigrant children's needs and to prepare mainstream teachers to cope with their new students. Hiring decisions were painful. Latino principals and teachers were scarce; mainstream teachers were tenured. Educators—as members of both the community and the wider society—reflected what Cortes (1986) has called the societal curriculum. They had internalized views and perceptions about change and about the challenge to California of educating a rapidly growing number of new immigrant students. Some teachers saw immigrant students as defenseless and as needing help and support. Others, however, saw them as intruders, as freeloaders, and as part of a group that simply refused to become American. They were strongly sympathetic to the activities of anti-immigrant groups in California that were actively beginning to promote a series of state initiatives that would directly impact on Latino immigrants

The feelings and the views of mainstream parents, school administrators, and teachers were widely shared by others in the town of Mission Vista as well as by many others in California. Concerns about immigrants—both legal and illegal—were increasing. To be fair, many of these worries and concerns were legitimate and valid. People had a right to ask such questions as: Have we lost control of our borders? Can this country support an unlimited number of new workers? Will native-born workers of all backgrounds (e.g., African American, Latino, European American) be displaced by persons willing to work for lower wages? Do new immigrants understand what it means to be American? Are they willing to learn English?

THE SCHOOL

The same uncertainties and concerns present in the community were played out in numerous ways in the schools. Nevertheless, Garden Middle School was a pleasant place. The buildings, while not new, had recently been painted. The grounds were clean, and the playing fields surrounding the school were well maintained. The classrooms were located in four separate one-story buildings. Each classroom had both a front and a back door, each opening to the patio area between each building. The main office, the attendance office, the multipurpose room, and the library were also located in separate but closely adjacent buildings.

Between classes students sat and talked on the patios or in the outside lunch area. Students enrolled in mainstream classes normally congregated together. This group included children of the original residents of the area—who were White, well dressed, and very much engaged in extracurricular activities—as well as students from Asia and India and even Latin America who were middle-class and had been here for many years.

This latter group of students was made up of fluent English speakers who seldom associated with the students who did not speak English.

Newly arrived immigrant students also kept mainly to themselves. Outside the classroom they spoke in Spanish to one another—sometimes loudly, sometimes in a whisper—and in certain ways mirrored the "American" behavior of their mainstream peers. Their dress, their demeanor, and their comportment, however, were not quite American. The girls either wore a little too much makeup and clothes that were a little too tight or they dressed very much like little children. The older boys strutted about ogling the girls and making the kinds of remarks to each other that they might have made on the streets of their towns in Mexico. The younger boys appeared to be shy and quiet and generally looked down respectfully when addressed by an adult. The most newly arrived youngsters looked uncomfortable. To outsiders they seemed shy and insecure.

As in other schools in which population shifts have rapidly changed the composition of the student body, there were tensions at Garden Middle School. The increasing number of non-English- or limited-English-speaking children had made demands on the staff and on the curriculum that had not been anticipated. Because of the increased enrollment of non-English-speaking children, the single ESL teacher had been joined by a colleague. Together, the two ESL teachers served every child in the school who was not yet fully fluent in English. Their classes generally enrolled 35 to 40 students.

Overall, the administration had worked hard to try to provide a program in which NEP[1] (non-English-proficient) and LEP (limited-English-proficient) children could have access to the curriculum. They had designed a NEP and LEP core in which these students received instruction in both ESL (English as a second language) and social studies, and they had made an effort to provide other "real" subject-matter courses for these students. While many of the teachers who had never worked with ELL students still did not want to work with them, it is noteworthy that a number of subject-matter teachers in science, math, and computers offered "sheltered" content classes[2] at different levels. Classes in science, math, and computers could be taken by NEP students who understood very little English. As might be imagined, the challenges faced by these content teachers were many.

During the years in which the study took place, Garden Middle School was a school in transition. It was a mainstream community's sole public middle school, a school where a few years earlier children of the neighborhood had felt comfortable and safe. Because of the population shift, this was changing. According to the former superintendent, the school was at the beginning of intensive "White flight." More and more middle-class parents were enrolling their children in private schools. They were afraid of the dropping standards, of the problems that might accompany non-English-background students, of gangs, of violence, and of interethnic romance.

In a very significant way, Garden Middle School is representative of schools all over the country that are changing as a result of the dramatic increase of "diverse" populations in many communities. Its almost all-White faculty had little experience with diversity. According to one teacher who worked closely with the Latino community, most teachers at Garden could predict few of the problems their "new" students would encounter. Most knew little about poverty. They had little notion of why working parents might not be able to make midday appointments with their children's teachers. They suspected lack of interest, apathy, and even antagonism and were baffled and troubled by the failure of these parents to "care" about their children.

The "new" students, on the other hand, did not quite yet know how to be American middle school students. They knew little about school spirit. They were not sure why being in the band or in chorus or in the computer club might be important. They frequently confused teachers' friendly demeanor with permissiveness, and they quickly found themselves in trouble. They understood little of what went on around them, and they often became discouraged and uninterested.

THE ESL PROGRAM AT GARDEN MIDDLE SCHOOL

The ESL program at Garden Middle School was divided into several levels including: (1) NEP, (2) LEP, (3) advanced LEP, and (4) sheltered English. All levels of the ESL program enrolled students in the sixth, seventh, and eighth grades. The program was traditional in orientation in that ESL was viewed as an academic subject that needed to be taught following a particular sequence organized around a grammatical syllabus.

The NEP core was designed for non-English-proficient students who had little or no background in English. It met for three periods a day and covered both ESL and social studies. The LEP core was designed for students who had some background in English and had been classified by the Idea Proficiency Test as limited-English-proficient. It met for only two periods a day and was taught as a high-beginner/low intermediate ESL course. The ESL course was complemented by a LEP social studies class. The advanced LEP core was designed for students who had some background in English and had been classified by the Idea Proficiency Test as advanced limited-English-proficient. It also met for two periods a day. The sheltered English core was a transitional course between the mainstream English-language courses and advanced LEP. It met for two periods a day and was taught by a half-time English teacher who believed strongly in the writing process.

In addition to the language courses per se, the following sheltered subject-matter courses were open to students in the program:

NEP sheltered science (grades 6, 7, 8)
NEP home arts (grades 7, 8)
NEP sheltered math (grades 6, 7, 8)
NEP sheltered computers (grades 6, 7, 8)
LEP science (grades 6, 7, 8)

These courses were taught, in English, by regular subject-matter teachers who had agreed to be part of the program. Each of the NEP sheltered courses had as a goal teaching subject matter (e.g., earth science, cooking, math) in English to students who were at zero or almost zero English. Administrators and a selected group of faculty were committed to giving students access to the normal middle school curriculum.

There was little mobility, however, between ESL levels. Few Latino students who entered Garden Middle School as low beginners in English ever reached advanced LEP. Even fewer were advanced to the sheltered English core or exited from the ESL program. Students enrolled in both advanced LEP and the sheltered English core were not the products of the Garden Middle School ESL program. They were students who had done academic work exclusively in English during their elementary school years but who were still not considered to be at the appropriate mainstream or non-ESL levels at Garden Middle School. Mainstream English teachers, we were told, were especially reluctant to have non-English-background students in their classes no matter what levels of proficiency they had reached. They worried particularly about the errors that were still present in their English-language production.

Placement and Assessment

One of the most challenging problems for Garden Middle School was the assessment of English-language proficiency in entering students. Placement in the ESL versus the mainstream classes depended directly on such assessment.

In California, students who enroll in a school for the first time are asked to complete a home language survey. This survey asks a series of yes/no questions in order to determine whether a language other than English is spoken at home and whether the student should be included in a language-assistance program. The survey is a screening procedure that allows school personnel to determine which children need to have their English-language proficiencies tested. In theory, all children whose home survey identifies them as speaking a language other than English at home must then be assessed using one of the state-approved instruments. This assessment is to be carried out as early as possible in the school year in order to ensure that students are given access to whatever language-assistance programs are available.

According to Macias and Kelly (1996), states generally use multiple criteria and methods to identify ELL students, including language-proficiency tests and home language surveys. The most commonly used tests include the Language Assessment Scales, the Idea Oral Language Proficiency Test, and the Language Assessment Battery. Factors taken into account include previous grades, referrals, scores on achievement tests (e.g., California Achievement Test [CAT], Comprehensive Tests of Basic Skills [CTBS], and Iowa Tests of Basic Skills [ITBS]), teacher observations, informal assessments, and criterion-referenced tests.

At Garden Middle School, placement in the ESL program depended on a number of factors. However, most students who stated on the home survey instrument that they came from homes where a language other than English was spoken were generally placed in the ESL sequence. In theory, the school used both home language surveys *and* an approved instrument to assess language proficiency and to place students in an appropriate program. In practice, however, because of the large number of students entering the school and because there was little time available between the time that students registered for school and the time school began, many students were placed in courses at Garden Middle School *before* their English-language proficiency was formally assessed. Students whose English had not been assessed by the school or district before, who were newly arrived, or who indicated that a non-English language was spoken at home were automatically placed in the NEP sequence. If it was later determined by the student's classroom performance or by the test—when it was finally administered—that he or she belonged at a higher level, that student was then moved to the appropriate classes in the sequence.

The IPT Test

The instrument used for assessing student proficiency was the IPT (Idea Oral Proficiency Test). The IPT was used to determine student levels of English proficiency as well as to monitor student progress. Designed to be administered and scored by school personnel, the version of the IPT test in use during the period of the study consisted of six score levels that were used to classify students as NES (non-English-speaking), LES (limited-English-speaking), and FES (fluent-English-speaking).

The IPT assesses students' listening comprehension ability (e.g., Point to the astronaut in the top left corner of the picture), grammar (What is the plural of *mouse*?), and vocabulary (What tool would you use to cut through wood?). To move from NES to LES, for example, students are expected to know the numbers up to 1,000, to be able to point to the appropriate clock when told the time of day, to be able to produce the comparative and superlative forms of regular adjectives, to give the appropriate verb form when given a particular pattern (e.g., Is he working? No, he *isn't*. Are they working? No, they *aren't*.), and to comprehend a short segment of connected discourse.

Like many other tests designed to assess English-language proficiency, the IPT provides a very superficial view of a student's actual academic language proficiency (August & Hakuta, 1997). There is no evidence, for example, that the particular tasks and questions included on the test actually reflect the demands made on students by a mainstream classroom setting. It is thus possible for students to score at the highest levels on this test and still not be able to comprehend and interpret texts used in their classes, to understand instructional discourse, to produce written texts, or to use oral language appropriately for academic purposes. Conversely, students can be classified as less proficient than they really are because they have not have studied the particular vocabulary tested (e.g., *hatchet, ax*) or because they have not learned or been taught grammatical terminology.

During the fall of the first year of the study, testing at Garden Middle School ran late because the school district was unwilling to hire substitute teachers for the many days that testing would require. Only the two ESL teachers were technically qualified to administer the test at Garden, and they were both overwhelmed by the very large number of students that had entered that year.

Test scores were taken very seriously by school personnel. Previous study of English and number of years of residence in this country were not weighted heavily in placement decisions. As a result, it was possible for a youngster who had been schooled totally in English in this country since the first grade to be placed in the ESL program. A youngster from a non-English-speaking background who, according to the IPT, did not test as FES was considered to be unable to learn new content taught in English. It did not matter that the student had already been reclassified or redesignated as fluent-English-speaking by another school or school district. Nor did it matter that a student had demonstrated ability to learn through English instruction during the elementary school years. Previous grades were not a key factor at Garden, nor were teacher recommendations.

Conversely, language assessment scores and classifications did not *by themselves* determine students' exit from the ESL program. Youngsters were not released from the program or placed at higher levels within the ESL sequence simply because of their scores on the IPT. Once *in* the program, placement was primarily determined by the teacher's judgment of a student's general performance on classroom tasks and assignments. For example, students who had not completed a particular textbook or who had poor grades on classroom tests of spelling and grammar were not permitted to advance further no matter how proficient they might otherwise seem in their use of English.

In addition to the IPT, students' general reading ability —or "literacy level"—was also tested using the Gates-MacGinitie Reading Test.[3] Unfortunately, the test offered little information about the L1 literacy levels of newly arrived students, whether highly literate in their first language or not. Tested in English, they simply scored as nonreaders.[4] To our knowledge, no assessments of first-language competencies (e.g., reading and writing abilities in Spanish) were made by the school. Additionally, little information was available to teachers about the educational levels attained by NEP students who were schooled in their home countries.

THE ESL TEACHERS AT GARDEN MIDDLE SCHOOL

The two ESL teachers at Garden Middle School were very different The senior teacher, Mrs. Clayton, had been at Garden for many years. A small red-haired woman who spoke flawed but comprehensible Spanish, she was an enthusiastic champion of those Mexican-background students whom she believed to be hardworking and motivated. She routinely contacted students' families to inform them of the kinds of things that she expected of their children, but she had little patience with behavior problems or with simple adolescent laziness. She ran a tight ship and closely followed an ESL textbook series that was grammar-based. Among her colleagues and school administrators, Mrs. Clayton had the reputation of being a good, traditional, no-nonsense teacher who had a difficult time responding to change.

The other ESL teacher, Mrs. Gordon, was a strikingly tall and elegant blonde in her early 30s who had taught English in Saudi Arabia for a number of years and who had learned some Spanish in college while an exchange student in Spain. Her assignment at Garden was her first experience in teaching ESL in an American public school. Her previous teaching experience in the United States had been at the elementary level, where she had implemented a literature-based curriculum with mainstream, English-speaking students.

There appeared to be some tensions between the two teachers. Mrs. Gordon complained that she could not change the program because of Mrs. Clayton, and Mrs. Clayton pointed out that what Latino students needed was discipline, not kindness. Ironically, although Mrs. Gordon was indeed pleasant and soft-spoken, Mrs. Clayton—gruff manner and all— was by far the favorite of the ELL students. She went out of her way to greet students during morning and lunch breaks; she inquired about brothers and sisters; she sent regards to mothers and fathers; she asked about student progress in other classes; and she made herself available for extra help. At evening functions when parents were present, Mrs. Clayton was usually surrounded by youngsters who wanted her to meet their mother or their father or to talk to their younger siblings. Mrs. Gordon, on the other hand, usually stood alone at these events or interacted exclusively with the other teachers present. From her remarks about her discomfort at such functions, we concluded that she was a very shy individual who was very uncertain about how to interact with newly arrived parents.

CHALLENGES AND REALITIES

Both ESL teachers were competent professionals who were committed to doing their best under very difficult circumstances. They had received very little training in second-language teaching, and they were responsible for too many students at too many different levels. Like many other teachers around the country, they did the best they could. They designed a sequence of courses, they set entry and exit criteria, and they chose a textbook series that focused on grammar. Filled with energy and determination, they set out to "teach" English.

Both teachers were aware of tensions in the community, of the isolation of the children in their neighborhoods, and of their own isolation as teachers of ELL learners. They understood that mainstream teachers largely viewed the ESL teachers' role as making certain that English language learners would be kept both out of the way and very busy. Given the school climate, they had little flexibility and very few allies.

School administrators, however, understood that, while they had made some progress, they had a long way to go. When I approached the principal and asked for permission to carry out the project, she was enthusiastic about what could be learned. At the suggestion of the principal, I met with the ESL teachers to explain the goals of the project and to describe the kinds of cooperation and involvement it would require. Because the school administration was eager to have us conduct the study, Mrs. Gordon agreed to allow me to identify four newly arrived Latino-background students in her classroom whom I might shadow for a 2-year period.

In the next chapter, I describe Mrs. Gordon's classroom and the ways in which newly arrived children "studied and learned" English. I offer details about classroom activities that—while well managed—seem very far from creating the acquisition-rich environment envisioned by second-language researchers. As I pointed out in Chapter 1, it is rare for L2 teachers to create such ideal environments in ordinary classroom settings, given the demands made on them by their institutions. What I saw in Mrs. Gordon's classroom was typical of the practices generally found in other middle school and high school ESL programs. In many ways, her class was superior to others I had observed in the area. As a researcher and part-time visitor, however, I cannot be certain that the activities that went on in my presence were actually the same activities that went on when I was not present. I begin Chapter 3, then, by raising questions about the nature of classroom research and by examining the dilemmas surrounding the observation of classroom practice by well-meaning researchers.

3

Teaching English at
Garden Middle School

As is the case with many other research projects that focus on student progress, much of what I wanted to know about English-language learners was closely tied to the kinds of instructional programs to which students had access. Understanding the development of English in both the oral and written modes in newly arrived students required me to carry out my work in classrooms—within what some researchers have referred to as the mysterious "black box" of school practice.

I chose the school where the study began quite deliberately. I knew of a few exemplary programs where outstanding instruction was being offered to English-language learners. I also knew that in most nonexemplary but highly typical programs, instructors struggled to meet the needs of a new population of students. I selected a nonexemplary setting knowingly in order to explore the academic success and failure of immigrant students in ordinary schools. In making this choice, I understood clearly that the challenge would involve being able to talk about the process of learning and not learning English in a less-than-ideal setting in a way that might inform future practice without indicting the performance of teachers of goodwill.

I was well aware that carrying out research in classrooms involves a number of difficulties and dilemmas. Sometimes, research is carried out jointly by both a researcher and a classroom teacher. In such cases, the researcher and the teacher together agree on the goals of the research, on the researcher's role in the classroom, and on the ways in which feedback about practice and the research process will be provided by both individuals. In other cases, such as my own, researchers—rather than collaboratively researching a practice and its effects—propose instead to study what *is*. They want to examine student performance in an instructional context that has not been directly influenced by the researcher.

The difficulties and dilemmas involving this latter kind of research and the entire question of influence have to do with the well-known observer's paradox. The observer's presence, in and of itself, transforms the context. Teachers, no matter how experienced, understand that the researcher does not arrive on the scene as a neutral observer. As Sarason (1996) pointed out, "It is a very rare observer who will not come to his or her task with a critical stance, who will not unreflectively define and literally place problems (defined by the observer or others) *within* schools and whose recommendations for change will not focus exclusively on internal practices and structures" (p. 15). Many university researchers visiting schools have a fundamental desire to change schools. They come—as I did—with what Sarason termed *shoulds* and *oughts* that are often barely disguised. While the teacher and researcher may, in the course of a project, develop a rapport that allows them to talk frankly about practice and research, I suspect that, in many cases, teachers struggle to give researchers what they want, while researchers struggle to assure teachers that they only want to see and understand the teacher's *genuine* practice. For the researcher, the greatest difficulty involves observing silently without comment. The temptation to intervene, to persuade, and to lead practitioners from darkness into light is overwhelming. The fact that the practice might be typical of most other instructional settings and representative of the kinds of instruction that have been widely criticized in the field creates even greater complexity.

Many educational researchers want in some way to contribute to change by carrying out research. They hope that by spending months or years in a school setting, they might be able to learn something that can be generalized to other settings, something that can make a difference in children's lives. Ironically, however, having decided to study nonexemplary settings, they have put themselves in a serious bind. The best they can do is to focus on those aspects of the practice that are common to other settings and to describe both their strengths and weaknesses. They must, however, clearly point out the limitations of what they saw as well as the possibility that teachers' practices—perhaps because they sought to obtain the researcher's approval—might not have been truly genuine.

It is important for me to point out, then, that the ESL teaching practices that are presented here, while common in many schools and classrooms, may not truly reflect Mrs. Gordon's actual practice. Mrs. Gordon was a teacher of goodwill who cared deeply about her students. She was faced by a number of challenges during the 2 years that I visited her classroom—not the least of which was my own presence.

MRS. GORDON'S ESL CLASSROOM

I began observations in Mrs. Gordon's classroom 2 weeks after school had begun. It was a typical California fall. The weather was warm, and students wore summer clothes to school. As is often the case at the beginning of the year, the school was at its best. Former students were eager to be back after a long summer, and teachers talked enthusiastically about their plans for the academic year.

As classroom visitors 2 days a week, my graduate assistant, Rosa Rodriguez, and I took on the roles of designated computer experts, as Mrs. Gordon had requested. We were asked to work individually with students, selected from a list provided to us, to introduce them to Kid Pix, a paint-and-draw program for young children, and teach them how to use the mouse on a MacIntosh computer. Computer time technically began during second period, when students broke up into groups to complete their seat-work. When Rosa and I were both in the classroom, one of us would circulate among the students and the other would work at the computer. During this time, we could also observe Mrs. Gordon during her small-group instruction—an activity that took place at the front of the room while other groups were engaged in seatwork.

For a period of some weeks, Mrs. Gordon frequently involved me in conversations about her teaching. I found it easy to find something to praise and generally commented about activities that seemed especially well done. I was not successful, however, in creating an interactional context in which discussions about ESL teaching in general could take place. I often found myself retreating, measuring my words, and fearing that she might misunderstand a general remark about language development as a criticism of her practice.

As the project unfolded, both Mrs. Gordon and I struggled to develop a closer working relationship. It was not easy. The students were a challenge, and the power differences between us were evident no matter how much I wanted to pretend that they did not exist. Personally, moreover, Mrs. Gordon was living through a very difficult period. Her mother was seriously ill and, because her parents lived in the southern part of the state, she spent many evenings and weekends on the road to and from her mother's. She was often tired and admitted to me that she was cranky.

Still, in spite of the difficulties, I believe that we both tried. Given the opportunity to start the project again, I would do many things differently. I suspect that she would, too. I take comfort in thinking that by writing about the challenges we both faced and about the difficulties of describing genuine classroom practices, we can both contribute in some way to a better understanding of the dilemmas that surround educational research.

The Students

The students who were part of the beginning ESL core from which Lilian, Elisa, Manolo, and Bernardo were selected were tall and short, fat and thin, neat and disheveled, and as young as 11 and as old as 14. Some boys had clearly grown to their full height and were typical adolescents in orientation. They paid much attention to the well-developed, sophisticated girls in the room who constantly fiddled with their hair and nails. Other boys and girls were still children. Twenty-eight of the thirty students in the beginning ESL core were Latino and Spanish-speaking. One was Japanese, and one was Taiwanese. All students sat four to a table for most of the activities during the three periods.

General Student Characteristics. There were many similarities and many differences among the students enrolled in the beginning ESL classroom. Some students had just arrived from Mexico or Central America during the summer. These students were, in general, better behaved than the others, a bit more quiet and attentive, and overall still somewhat unsettled. Many of them were extremely homesick and eagerly talked about their old school, their old neighborhood, and the grandparents and other relatives they had left behind. Some sat in their seats woodenly, not participating. Others watched the more "established" students carefully, often imitating their behavior closely. The newly arrived students were almost without exception at zero English.

Other students, however, seemed to function to some degree in English. They clearly understood what the teacher said and could respond in a chorus to the questions asked of the entire class. From our observations of these latter students over the course of the year, we concluded that these students who were not at zero English constituted two major groups: (1) those students who were considered behavior problems and had been placed in the beginning ESL class as a punitive measure in spite of their proficiency in English and (2) those whose English still showed many limitations but who varied immensely in terms of their proficiencies. Many students in this latter group had been in this country since the elementary school years, while others had been here only a year or two. Many of the seventh- and eighth-graders in this group had been in the beginning ESL class at Garden the previous year. We later learned that the "normal" path at Garden for all but the most outstanding students was to spend 2 years in the beginning class (with a different teacher each year) and a final year in the intermediate class. Few students moved to the advanced ESL class, and even fewer ever exited from the ESL program.

Federico and Sergio, for example, were typical "punitive ESL" students. Federico wore dark baggy clothes and rarely spoke. When told to do something, he sat still and did not respond. The teacher usually repeated her request several times. I was told that he was a habitual truant of about 15, a gang member or gang wannabe, and a student other youngsters feared and respected. No one appeared to know how long he had been in the United States, but it was evident—even from his studied lack of response—that he understood English well. Sergio, on the other hand, was a mischievous, outgoing troublemaker who was constantly talking. In order to control his behavior, the teacher had isolated him in the back of the room. Nevertheless, he insisted on responding to all questions asked of the entire class in a very loud voice. He could function quite well in English and could use this language to annoy and even to ridicule the teacher.

I was not immediately able to determine exactly why these students were retained at the beginning level. I conjectured that the testing instruments that were used in the school were not sensitive to particular kinds of growth and development. I later learned that, because the ESL teachers at Garden wanted to conduct ESL classes entirely in English, they depended on students who already understood the language to translate and interpret for newly arrived youngsters.

The Focal Students. After a 1-month period during which we observed those students who appeared to meet the study's criteria, I selected six students for initial in-depth study. Of these six students, four appeared to be literate in Spanish at age-appropriate levels. Two others appeared to have had more limited educational backgrounds. I had intended to make a final selection of four students at the end of the semester. Unfortunately, one student did not fill out the required forms and two others left Garden before the Christmas break. As a result, a newly arrived youngster who met the study's criteria was added to the remaining original three focal students. This youngster, Bernardo Salas, was selected because he was from an urban area close to Mexico City and because he had been a student at the *secundaria* level. Students who have completed their basic education (*primaria*) spend two years in *secundaria* (lower secondary level) before entering *preparatoria* (the upper secondary level). Since many children of ordinary families drop out within the first three years of school, working-class students who persist and enroll in *secundaria* are considered exceptional. Bernardo was the closest substitute available for the originally selected student with a strong educational background.

In sum, the final selection of focal students involved many months of observations at Garden School. Characteristics of the four students as determined at the time of selection are shown in Table 3.1.

Table 3.1. Characteristics of Focal Students

Characteristics	Students
Schooled in a rural area	Elisa, Lilian
Schooled in an urban or largely urban area	Manolo, Bernardo
High literacy skills	Bernardo
Medium literacy skills	Manolo, Elisa
Low literacy skills	Lilian
Parents knew some English	Manolo, Elisa
Parents knew only Spanish	Lilian, Bernardo
Sixth-grade students	Manolo, Bernardo
Seventh-grade students	Lilian, Elisa

Three Periods of ESL

Mrs. Gordon's NEP core was scheduled for the first three periods of the day, beginning at 8:00 A.M. and ending at 10:38. Morning activities began with students coming into the classroom and taking their seats at "tables" of four to six students. After the bell rang, Mrs. Gordon expected students to sit quietly and to listen to announcements as they came in over the public address system. When the announcements were finished, classroom activities began with a salute to the flag and a student volunteer announcing the day's date.

Working with the Entire Class

For the greater part of the year, the teacher would work with the entire class during the beginning of the first period. She spoke rapidly in English about general activities coming up (e.g., parent–teacher conferences, school games, books that could be ordered through the *Weekly Reader* program, contributions to the Thanksgiving food drive). These remarks were generally aimed at the mid- and high-level NEP students who had some comprehension abilities in English. No attempt was made to adjust the level of English, to provide some type of advance organizer that would allow the very beginning students to have a sense of what to listen for, or to use these presentations to have students develop strategies in listening comprehension. From time to time, one of the beginning students would whisper a question in Spanish to a more fluent student about the teacher's remarks. Mrs. Gordon would stop her presentation and remark, "I do not hear silence."

Running a Tight Ship

Hearing silence appeared to be very important to Mrs. Gordon. For example, she did not tolerate the volunteering of answers when she asked a question of the entire class. Each student was expected to respond only when called on. Talking was also discouraged between activities when students moved from their seats to work with Mrs. Ayub, the instructional aide, at her workstation or with Mrs. Gordon at the table. Interaction was also discouraged among students who remained at their seats. Even though the desks were set up to form working tables of four to six students, no group activities involving collaboration were assigned. Students were expected to work silently on their own.

Correcting Sentences

The second activity of the day involved punctuation and spelling and focused on days of the week and dates. At the start of the day, Mrs. Gordon would write sentences such as the following on the board:

> To die is thurzday Ocrober 3rd!
> ToMorrow WILL be Friday November 2? 1,9,96,
> Yesterday was Wednesday the 23rd of October

When the punctuation and spelling activity began, students would raise their hands and volunteer to correct one error at a time. Most students in the class tended to participate in this activity. Mrs. Gordon gave a lot of positive feedback to each student who walked up to the board and corrected an error successfully. Toward the latter part of the year, this activity expanded to include eliciting punctuation rules from students. Normally, Mrs. Gordon would offer the frame that would allow students at the very beginning level to state the rule:

> *Teacher*: You put a period there because it's the end of what?
> *Students*: Of a sentence?
> *Teacher*: Yes, very good.

The corrected sentences would remain on the board until the next day.

Small-Group Instruction

During the language segment of the instructional period, Mrs. Gordon and Mrs. Ayub both worked with small groups of students while other students worked at their tables. Groups were given names (e.g., Little Condors, White Rabbits, Strong Tigers), reflecting Mrs. Gordon's previous teaching experience in the early grades. Instruction during this time involved the teaching of structure (e.g., use *when* in a sentence) and vocabulary (e.g., use *living room* in a sentence). A flip chart of "minitests" focusing primarily on structure was located next to the table where this small-group instruction took place.

On the days when we were present, students did not engage in activities designed to develop their ability to use language to carry out functions, such as asking and answering genuine questions; conducting short, routine conversations; expressing needs, feelings, and ideas; getting personal needs met; developing relations with others; and engaging in transactions. Even though the textbook included a number of activities and communicative exercises designed to develop such abilities, instruction focused exclusively on the grammatical points included in each chapter.

Group instruction for the lowest-ability group was carried out by Mrs. Ayub, who focused on vocabulary. With very beginning students she used the "IDEA" box (a box of flash cards of vocabulary which is part of the curriculum available to support the IPT used in the school to assess English-language development). In working with students, Mrs. Ayub would generally hold up cards, point to the picture, and say the English word. Students were expected to repeat it. At later stages, she held up cards and expected individual students to say the English word by themselves. Occasionally, Mrs. Ayub tried to expand beyond the pronunciation of a single word and attempted to use the target words in meaningful sentences. Words belonging to very different topic areas were introduced at the same time (e.g., seasons of the year, pieces of furniture, numbers). The sentence examples produced by Mrs. Ayub were also unrelated. Since neither translations nor illustrations were used in these activities, it was not clear that beginning students understood the examples or the words being drilled. The illustrations on the cards were often ambiguous. Most students usually listened passively and repeated words (as opposed to sentences) when told to do so.

Seatwork

Seatwork involved a number of activities, including direct work on language as well as work on social studies activities. This type of work took place when Mrs. Gordon and Mrs. Ayub instructed the small groups as well as at various other times. Students each had a folder containing work that they were to complete during these periods. Different students worked with different materials. The beginning students primarily engaged in coloring and copying sentences from worksheets. Newly arrived students and students who came into the classroom later in the year were given mimeo sheets that had pictures of objects. Students would examine a picture, fill in the blank in each sentence (e.g., This is a boy), and color the picture. Students were expected to copy the English sentence and to carefully color the accompanying small picture of the object in question. For reasons we did not entirely understand, coloring was highly valued as an activity; both Mrs. Gordon and Mrs. Ayub considered it valuable for newly arrived students to color many small pictures. They were under the impression that most of these students had missed an important developmental step because they had not colored as children. In any event, coloring small pictures took up a great deal of time and otherwise kept students—whose English was so low that they could not profit from other activities—quite busy. It was not clear, however, whether students understood what they were writing in English or how to say the words that they were writing.

More advanced students working at their seats also copied sentences. These students, however, normally copied from the workbook accompanying the class text. Sentences included structures such as the following: The man has a brown hat. The boy lives in the house. The hat is on the chair. As was the case with the beginning students, it was not obvious to us that the students knew how to pronounce the segments that they were writing or what they meant. When we circulated around the room, we often overheard students whispering explanations and definitions to each other in Spanish.

Work on Social Studies Activities

Social studies activities during the year focused on two main themes: a map and map-reading unit and a national parks unit. Most of the work in each of the units was carried out as seatwork activity after the teacher gave brief directions to the entire class on what the worksheet materials required.

Map activity, for example, required students to examine a map of the town of Mission Vista, to find their homes on the map, and to color streets using different-colored crayons. At the beginning of the activity, much time was taken up in passing out boxes of crayons to each table. Much whispering and giggling went on at these times.

Instructions about a particular worksheet activity were often difficult to understand for a number of students. On one occasion, for example, the task involved learning to measure distances on a map using a scale. Rulers and dittos were passed out. Each inch on the map was intended to represent 100 feet, and students had to measure a number of distances. The teacher repeated the instructions several times, held up the ditto, and held up the ruler. At the tables, students whispered to each other. There was much confusion.

Reading to the Entire Class

[handwritten annotation: elementary methods — pictures hard to see — no comprehensible input — no teaching]

After the morning break, Mrs. Gordon was quite fond of reading aloud to the entire class using children's illustrated books from her days at the elementary school level. During an entire month, for example, she read to the students from children's books about baboons and capuchin monkeys. The books were truly delightful pop-up books that would probably have interested students even as old as those in the sixth, seventh, and eighth grades had they been able to handle the books themselves. Mrs. Gordon read from the books and held them up from time to time for students to see. Most students sitting in the room had a hard time (as did we) in making out the pictures.

As a comprehensible input activity, supported by pictures designed to increase students' understanding of spoken language, the book reading was less than totally successful. Most students in the room probably understood little beyond the fact that she was talking about monkeys. However, the high-level beginners did indeed appear to comprehend some of the extended discourse she provided in her comments about what she had read. They responded to her questions:

> *Teacher*: Where do capuchin monkeys live?
> *Students*: In trees.

Filling up Extra Time

Another favorite activity for Mrs. Gordon was the game traditionally known as "hangman" but which she softened by calling it "hang-the-spider." We witnessed the playing of this game almost every time we visited the class. Typically, this was a full-class activity in which Mrs. Gordon used vocabulary words from a familiar topic. Often, but not always, this vocabulary was drawn from the social studies material. In playing the game, Mrs. Gordon drew the typical hangman structure and wrote the first and last letters of the word to be guessed by the students. Students raised their hands to respond and were generally scolded for talking out of turn. Guesses of the entire word were not permitted.

In terms of English-language development, this activity seemed to be accessible even to the least proficient students. By participating in the game, these students could potentially learn the names of the letters. It is not evident, however, that students gained much from the game as a vocabu-

lary exercise. Because the words picked for the game often came from different areas and topics, students did not always know what the various words meant. They participated in the game by simply guessing letters and did not appear to be particularly concerned about the meaning of words.

Eliciting Language

Occasionally Mrs. Gordon would attempt to involve students in whole-class interaction, mainly focusing on vocabulary. Very few of the students participated, and she tended to rely on two or three students to respond to her questions. A Halloween word-elicitation activity was typical of such interactions.

> *Teacher*: Okay, what is orange? It is a . . .
> *Student 1*: Uh . . .
> *Teacher*: Orange is a what? Is it an animal, a food, a color, or . . .
> *Student 2*: It's a color.
> *Teacher*: (*writes word on board*) Who else has a word? Rudolfo?
> *Student 3*: Cat.
> *Teacher*: OK, and cat is what?
> *Student 1*: Animal.
> *Teacher*: (*writes on board*) What kind of cat do we think of when . .
>
> *Student 2*: Black cat, a black cat.
> *Teacher*: A black cat. (*writes on board*) OK, what else? Larry?
> *Student 1*: Trick or treat.
> *Teacher*: OK. (*writes on board*) When do you use trick or treat?
> *Student 2*: (unintelligible)
> *Teacher*: Right. It's what you say to the people who open the door, isn't it? When you go from house to house. Yako?
> *Student 4*: Witch.

As was the case with such language-elicitation activities, the Halloween word activity went on for a period of about 35 minutes. In this particular case, given the topic of Halloween (which was new and exciting to many of the newly arrived students), most students paid close attention. Toward the end, Mrs. Gordon abandoned the strict elicitation question followed by one-word responses and provided comments and explanations designed to be understood by the beginning level students and also provided information about jack-o'-lanterns.

Teacher: OK, Yako.
Student 4: Jack-o-lantern.
Teacher: Jack-o'-lantern, OK. I'll put that over here. What's the difference between a pumpkin and a jack-o'-lantern?
Students: (whisper)
Teacher: What's the difference between them. There is a difference between the two. Juan?
Student 2: The jack-o'-lantern gots both uh eyes and mouth and nose, and the pumpkin doesn't have nothing.
Teacher: Exactly. The pumpkin is the big orange vegetable, all right? that grows in the garden, but the jack-o'-lantern is after you have cut it. So (*draws it on the board*) there's the pumpkin, right? after you have—Juan will you stop playing. That noise is irritating . . . thank you. You take your pumpkin and you carve (*draws*) out your face. That would be the jack-o'-lantern. *Lantern* means "light," doesn't it? So what are they saying is going to happen? What are you going to put inside there?

As will be noted, this interaction contains some examples of extensions of students' brief responses by the teacher. It also illustrates the teacher's efforts to engage students in an interesting activity by focusing on a topic of immediate widespread interest and providing, along with the elicitation of vocabulary, important cultural information about Halloween. In general, newly arrived students could not understand the teacher's more extensive explanations or comments. No advance organizers were provided, and no checks for comprehension were made.

Learning to Read in English *Little time spent Special Ed materials*

The teaching of reading did not take up much classroom time. During the entire year, we witnessed little instruction on reading itself. On one occasion, students did work as a class on deciphering *Scholastic News*, a weekly newspaper intended for elementary school children. In this particular case, the teacher went over the vocabulary found in the back of the newsletter. Only a few students could respond to her questions on what words such as *cap*, *gather*, and *college* meant. The class then moved to a hang-the-spider activity in which the teacher used vocabulary from the newsletter.

Reading, however, did take place. Essentially, mid- and high-level NEP students were expected to work independently with several sets of the *Barnell-Loft Readers*, a series of English-language readers developed for special education students. These materials are not intended for ESL learners and assume native-speaker abilities in English. Multiple-choice questions, for example, expect that students will have a large passive English-language vocabulary. At the lowest level, the *Barnell-Loft Readers* generally include brief passages accompanied by illustrations; at the higher levels, no illustrations are included. Each of the levels focuses students on particular kinds of reading (reading for main idea, guessing meaning in context, etc.). All readings are brief, and all questions are multiple-choice.

In Mrs. Gordon's class, the mid- to high-level NEP students used a teacher-designed answer sheet to enter their answers and to keep a record of their progress. Unfortunately, given their limited English, students learned little from marking wrong answers to multiple-choice questions. The teacher did not go over wrong answers and did not provide a way for students to discover whether they had been confused by the reading itself or by the wording of the multiple-choice questions. Only the highest-level students progressed beyond the first-level readers.

Learning to Write in English

Instruction in writing in Mrs. Gordon's NEP class was influenced by the fact that I entered her classroom having expressed a particular interest in the development of writing abilities in ESL students. I stressed that I simply wanted to examine how students progressed over time given the demands placed on them by the ESL class and by their subject-matter classes.

In general, Mrs. Gordon's NEP students produced writing by using *guided composition* strategies. Because Mrs. Gordon was particularly concerned about grammatical errors, she tried to guide students into producing sentences that were grammatically correct. In order to do so, she involved students in a very controlled process in which she gave a frame such as:

Capuchin monkeys   _____

and a set of elements that could be placed in the blank. For the capuchin monkey piece, for example, the following elements were written on the board:

breaking nuts on branches
live in the jungle in trees
live in South America
medium size monkeys
can jump from one tree to another
black and white monkeys

As will be apparent from the above example, students at the mid and high NEP levels who could manipulate these basic structures by adding needed

elements actually produced grammatically correct sentences. Low-level students, however, simply copied the structures and produced questionable
sentences, such as:

> Capuchin monkeys breaking nuts on branches.
> Capuchin monkeys black and white monkeys

When there was little interest in the topic, activities such as this produced
little frustration. On the other hand, when students really had something
to say or wanted to attempt to say something real, they found this approach to writing very frustrating. On Halloween, for example, Mrs. Gordon gave a writing assignment that asked students to write about what
they would do on Halloween night and how they would dress. She wrote
the following list of words on the board:

pirate
Bart Simpson
bird
ghost
Madonna
cat
rabbit
Jason
pumpkin
princess
turkey
skeleton
ninja
monkey

Below, and to the side of this list, she added a sentence starter (I want to
be) and several options as follows:

> I want to be

> go to a haunted house
> go to a cemetery
> go to a Halloween party
> go trick or treating

Although she orally modeled two sentences, "I want to be a princess" and
"I want to go trick or treating," the information on the board did not

provide students with an explanation about how to adjust the structure of
the sentence starter (I want to be) to form sentences expressing where they
wanted to go.

Lost a
teaching
moment

    That day at school many students in the mainstream classes and many
teachers were wearing costumes. Students were excitedly talking among
themselves and fantasizing about what they would like to be. In completing
the writing assignment, then, frustration was quite high. As we circulated
among the tables, we were asked how to say and how to spell many things
that were not on Mrs. Gordon's list. Respectful of the no-Spanish rule im-
posed in the classroom, we attempted to respond in English. We called out
letters in English. When I was overheard giving the correct spelling of a word
to one student, however, the teacher intervened and asked me to make the
student "sound it out." She went on to explain that she graded students on
both their accuracy and their effort. Although I would have liked to pursue
the topic to discover exactly how she viewed the process of sounding out for
second-language students, I did not consider it wise to do so.

    Overall, controlled writing activities resulted in almost identical papers
written by the different members of the class. These products, rather than
being written in paragraph form, consisted of a list of numbered sentences
such as the following two samples, which were produced at the end of the
year for the national parks reports:

THE GRAND TETONS
1. I say a moose in the movie.
2. There are mountains
3. There is two elk were fighting.
4. I saw snow on mountains.
5. We saw snow on trees.
6. We saw snow on the ground
7. There is flying ducks.

THE GRAND TETONS
1. The Grand Tetons are very big.
2. Two elks were fighting.
3. The Grand Tetons are nex to the Yellowstone National Park
4. I saw a valley in the park.
5. I saw a moose in a lake.
6. I saw duks flying.
7. I saw snow on trees.

In Mrs. Gordon's class, the development of writing abilities was seen
as a very controlled process in which students slowly learned how to write

individual sentences using correct grammar and vocabulary. The focus of the activity was both form *and* correctness. Like many ESL teachers, Mrs. Gordon had received no training in process writing. She did not believe in multiple drafts, in free writing, in brainstorming, or in any other techniques that might have moved the students' focus from form to meaning. She was not bothered by the fact that all her students wrote similar papers, many of which actually had identical sentences.

The English-Only Policy

When visiting the classroom, we often walked around the tables and helped to answer student questions about the activity. Because most students (especially the focal students) were aware that both Rosa and I spoke Spanish, we were often addressed in this language. At the beginning, we responded in Spanish as well. Mrs. Gordon, however, strongly objected to the use of Spanish in her classroom and stated that students tended to become lazy and made little effort to learn English if they were spoken to in Spanish. In order to comply with her policy on language, we attempted to speak English as much as possible.

A NEW TEACHER

During the winter quarter, Mrs. Gordon took a leave of absence to care for her mother. Fortunately for the project—because of the contrast it provided—we had the opportunity of observing another teacher work with the very same students during a 10-week period.

Mrs. Davidson was in every possible sense the direct opposite of Mrs. Gordon. Short, very plump, dark-haired, and enthusiastic, Sandra Davidson exuded confidence and enthusiasm. Not a trained ESL teacher, she was at the school as a temporary art instructor. She cared very much about writing and had spent a year working with Mrs. Perry, another teacher in the school district who—at the elementary school level—had implemented a showcase program in "accelerated literacy" for LEP students. Mrs. Perry (also not a trained ESL specialist) was very successful in making English-language writers out of Latino students whom other teachers considered to be in need of very structured ESL—not instruction in process writing. The experience of viewing limited- and non-English speakers as potential writers of English who could be taught using the many strategies currently popular with native-English-speaking children deeply colored the way in which Mrs. Davidson approached Mrs. Gordon's NEP class.

As did Mrs. Perry in her elementary accelerated literacy class, Mrs. Davidson made available stories and poetry to the NEP children. She expected them not only to appreciate the writing but also to produce such stories and poems themselves. Instead of worksheets, she gave students time to work on their rough drafts, to talk to each other in Spanish about their writing, to revise their drafts, and finally to enter their final product into the computer. These products varied in sophistication and correctness but seemed to reflect students' attempts to create real meaning. Two samples of such products are included here:

ENGLISH

Is ugly to swiniming. There are many bird different kind a birds. Like eagle and puffins like to see the ocean pacific. The sky and you can heat the echo in the mountains and the birds there noisy and the ocean.
            End

THE PUFFIN

Puffin is a animal the color black white and the mouth is color yellow and read in the rock in group of birds and eat a fish and incect.

Students appeared to enjoy the experience of writing, entering their writing into the computer, and pasting into the text illustrations of different types. Mrs. Davidson posted many of these products on the wall.

There were many differences between the products that students wrote under Mrs. Gordon's direction and those they produced when writing for Mrs. Davidson. As opposed to the firmly controlled correctness of the guided composition products, the process approach to writing resulted in writing in which the meaning of the entire segment was frequently difficult to understand. Moreover, writing and editing took a very long time. Not all students, for example, finished even one final draft of a written product. Students, however, were offered a new view of writing. They were each given a journal, and they each were expected to write in their journals every day.

A Different ESL Classroom

The experience of changing teachers in the middle of the schoolyear was not easy for either the students or the two teachers. Students missed Mrs. Gordon and often responded negatively to Mrs. Davidson's style. They were not used to reading aloud in class. They were not used to being expected to find answers to worksheets in real textbooks. But Mrs. Davidson did not know about the students' "limitations," and she proceeded to treat them as though they were middle school students who could learn subject matter as well as English. Her social studies unit, for example, focused on the missions in California. She expected students to find the missions on the map, to answer questions about the history of the different missions, and to respond enthusiastically in a chorus to her questions. As opposed to Mrs. Gordon, Mrs. Davidson did not like a quiet room. She liked noise, activity, and talk.

The instructional aide, Mrs. Ayub, not surprisingly was very ill at ease during this period. From time to time she would inform Mrs. Davidson that "these students" could not do this or that activity. For example, she objected strongly to an activity that involved students in coloring the entire map of the United States. She expressed surprise at the fact that Mrs. Davidson had not given students explicit instructions about what color they should use to color which parts of the map.

From a language-acquisition perspective, much of what Mrs. Davidson did intuitively was right on target. She provided access to the language, and she provided real content that needed to be discussed in the language that students were trying to learn. From a traditional ESL perspective, however, Mrs. Davidson, as compared to Mrs. Gordon, knew little about how to actually "teach" English. Small-group instruction on grammar took place infrequently, for example, and she made fewer distinctions between the low-, mid-, and high-ability NEP students.

The Special Case of Juana *Beginners*

In spite of her many strengths, Mrs. Davidson became almost overwhelmed when a new student who had had no previous schooling in Mexico was put into her classroom. For a period of several weeks, Juana became the focus of tensions and disagreements between Mrs. Ayub and Mrs. Davidson. Mrs. Ayub was content to sit the student at a table and have her classmates teach her how to color. Mrs. Davidson, on the other hand, wanted to do more. She instructed Mrs. Ayub to record vocabulary for Juana using a special card recorder and reader. With this machine, Juana could then sit and push individual cards into the machine, see the picture on the card, and hear the English word. This activity required that Mrs. Ayub record words using another special machine, cut out both a picture and a matching written word, and paste both of these on the "prerecorded" card. Mrs. Ayub, who had many other things to do, did not agree that recording vocabulary for one student was a good use of her time.

Both Rosa and I volunteered to help with Juana on the days when we were present in class. In the course of working with Juana, it became clear that, although she had not attended school, this 14-year-old girl had been taught a number of things at home by her mother. For example, she could count to 50 in Spanish and to 10 in English. She could her write her name, and she seemed very eager to learn. Unfortunately, our visits were not frequent enough to truly help either Juana or the two teachers. Indeed, we concluded that, in some ways, we may have made the situation worse.

One day, for example, I found when I arrived that Mrs. Davidson had decided to have Juana work on phonics worksheets that involved the sounds of the English vowels. Juana was sitting at her desk, head bowed, staring at the sheet. I looked to see what was expected and found that the first activity involved circling the capital and lowercase *a*'s. Mrs. Ayub had not been able to make clear to Juana what she wanted.

Juana quickly began to work when I explained what to do. The second worksheet, however, required her to circle long and short vowel sounds in animal and other object names. This activity assumed that she knew the English names of the animals pictured on the page, which included *ape*, *alligator*, and others. Juana did not know the names of the animals in English or know that English has two different sounds for the letter *a* called short *a* and long *a*.

What I decided to do, therefore, in order to figure out what kind of instruction might be appropriate, was to ask her how much she knew about letters. I learned that she could identify all the letters by their Spanish names.

In an attempt to see how quickly she might learn, I then wrote out consonant and vowel combinations in Spanish, such as *ba, be, bi, bo, bu, da, de, di, do, du*, and asked her to notice that the vowel sounds always stayed the same, while each letter said its name. She quickly caught on to the ways in which the sounds blended. I wrote out high-frequency words such as *Memo, dedo, casa, gato, pato, papa, mama*, which she immediately read back to me. It appeared that Juana had an excellent memory. When she got confused, she didn't always know which sounding-out strategy to use, but she was trying. Toward the end, I had her recognizing quite a few words. She was delighted and was disappointed when I had to stop.

In the meantime, Mrs. Ayub looked worried. She interrupted our activity several times and asked me to work with colors or with opposites. She kept trying to give me cards of isolated vocabulary words. She became quite nervous because I appeared to be teaching Juana to read in Spanish. I explained that Juana could be helped by grasping the concept of how letters and sounds are connected in her first language. Hearing our conversation, Mrs. Davidson came over, and I explained what I was doing. Embarrassed because I was implying that Juana could not work with the worksheets that had been chosen for her, she scolded Mrs. Ayub for not having worked harder in producing more cards for the sound machine.

I understood that I had overstepped my boundaries, and I quickly retreated and apologized. What I realized, however, is how lost they both were, how they had no understanding of beginning reading, and how nearly impossible it was for teachers to work with non-English-speaking children and children who had very limited literacy skills in their first language. While it was clear to me that Juana learned very fast and that it would not take very long at all to get her reading in Spanish, I also knew that what Juana required was either a one-on-one tutorial or a class in beginning literacy for Spanish-speaking students.

As it turned out, Juana's presence at Garden School was very brief indeed. Two weeks later, she and her twin brothers had left the school. Mrs. Ayub commented that the family had moved to another city in the area.

If Juana's presence is significant, it is because it highlighted the many difficulties encountered by teachers of goodwill and dedication who are, nevertheless, not equipped to deal with illiterate children. Sandra Davidson was a dedicated professional whose attitude toward the NEP students was both positive and encouraging. But faced with a Juana, she quickly reached the limits of her experience. She did not have the luxury of sitting one-on-one as I did to try to bring a single child to understand the relationship between print and sound. She had an aide who was ultimately loyal to the "real" classroom teacher, who was not a native speaker of English, and who did not speak the language of the students who were most at risk.

MRS. GORDON'S RETURN

By the end of the quarter, Mrs. Gordon was back in her own classroom. Hang-the-spider returned, as did controlled writing. The Little Condors were called up to work at the front table, and the low-level students went back to coloring and doing worksheets at their tables. A new student from El Salvador was placed by the window where he could work by himself with the cards and the sound machine. In her small group, Mrs. Gordon could be overheard asking: "What is an armchair?" "Who can make a sentence with *armchair*?" "What is a comic book?" "What happens when you read a comic book?" "Who can give me a sentence with *drinking*?"

The students were delighted. Three of our focal students commented that they had missed her. They all said that they liked her much more than they did Mrs. Davidson. The first day, the entire class was a little noisy. Students forgot to raise their hand when they wanted to say something, and they tended to volunteer answers. Mrs. Gordon patiently reminded them that in her class it was important to hear silence.

4

Lilian

Lilian was a blonde and blue-eyed, strikingly pretty youngster. At the beginning of the study, she was 12, mature for her age, and quite aware of her effect on the young male students in her class. The village from which Lilian came is a small one, and Lilian had never traveled even to the county seat a few miles away. In Mexico, this 12-year-old had been a little girl. She played, and ran, and went to school. She did not consider herself to be a budding adolescent. She was very homesick when we first talked, and she missed the smells of her village as well as her friends. Lilian was the third child in a family that included a 17-year-old brother, a 14-year-old sister, and 10-year-old twin brothers. Since their arrival in the United States, Lilian's mother, Sonia, had given birth to a new baby girl.

Lilian and her family lived in a particularly crowded apartment complex on a short dead-end street. The street was full of old cars, and often clusters of men stood outside one or another of the buildings. These were the men who had not found work that day and were passing time standing around, filling in the empty hours. The Duque family lived in a three-bedroom apartment that was shared by two families and other relatives. This included Lilian's family of eight, her father's brother and his wife and child, and two adult male cousins who were single. A total of 13 persons shared a single bathroom.

Lilian's father, Tito, had been in the United States for almost 10 years. He was here legally and worked for a gardening service. Tito's life had been that of a "cyclical migrant." Over a number of years he had gone back and forth to Mexico, spending several seasons in his village and then returning to work in northern California.

The summer before the study began, Tito was finally able to bring his entire family to the Bay Area. The new baby was born a few months after Mrs. Duque arrived, and the older children were soon enrolled in school. The children, however, had not lived with their father in a very long time. They were not used to his authority and to the tensions between their parents. Tito, in turn, had little experience in parenting three adolescents in a context in which he had little power. Needless to say, there were many tensions and problems in the family.

Sonia, Lilian's mother, had Lilian's same pretty face and light complexion. She was a friendly woman in her mid-30s who after only a few short months here began to understand how different life in California was from life in Mexico. She learned, for example, that her husband's salary—which in Mexico had seemed a fortune—could not stretch to pay the $800-dollar-a-month rent for the apartment. Although it made her unhappy, she understood that the family had to rent out part of its space in the small apartment in order to make ends meet. She also understood that, unwilling though she was to leave her young baby, she, too, needed to work outside the home. For many months, she tried desperately to find work. But Sonia knew little English, and there was not much that she could do. Finally, through a neighbor, she found work with a woman who had a house-cleaning service and who would hire teams of two women to clean three or four houses in a single day. After many months of working for the same service, Sonia still made $5 for each of the houses that she cleaned. Whenever a problem arose in the family that required her presence at home, Sonia sent her oldest daughter to clean in her place. To the woman who ran the house-cleaning service, excuses were unacceptable. If Sonia did not work or provide an acceptable substitute, she would be fired.

Throughout the period of the study, the demands on Sonia were extraordinary. She worked, took care of most of the household jobs, and tried to teach her children good moral values. She worried about Lilian's older sister, who had fallen in love with a newly arrived Mexican man; about her twins; and about her oldest son, who frequently got into fights. Life in Mexico had not prepared her to deal with Mission Vista. She felt guilty that she was letting her children down, that she did not know how to help them, and that she did not have time to go to school and to learn English. But Sonia was very sure about what she wanted for her daughters: She wanted them to make better choices than she had when choosing a husband. She was eager to have both Lilian and her sister Graciela work where they might meet young men with better futures, men who would not have to struggle as much as Tito did to support a family.

IN THE CLASSROOM

In the classroom, surrounded by her peers, Lilian was always hard to miss. She was different because of coloring, but she was also different because of her behavior. As opposed to most of the other Latina girls in her class,

Lilian did not try to pretend to be shy and demure. She pouted, tapped her fingers impatiently, and glared at the other girls across the room. Nothing about her demeanor suggested fear or insecurity. She appeared tough and ready to take on the world.

In the early weeks of the first year, however, when I observed her, I could see that she watched everyone carefully before she herself made a move. She was guarded and cautious and did not want to be wrong. When Mrs. Gordon gave directions to the whole class, Lilian—pretending indifference or boredom—would look to see what others were doing. Only when she was quite sure of what the activity involved would she begin to work. Typically, she worked slowly, keeping a careful eye on the papers of her tablemates. She rarely asked them for help and seemed to have little tolerance for their comments or helpful suggestions. "Ya sé" ("I already know"), she would snap when a classmate attempted to explain an assignment or to indicate that she had not quite understood. Very rarely would she volunteer to correct punctuation errors on the board during the beginning morning activity. From time to time, however, she would raise her hand during hang-the-spider and make an attempt to guess the next letter in the target word. It appeared, however, that Lilian either did not pay close attention to this activity or did not quite understand the talk surrounding the game. On more than one occasion, she proposed a letter that had already been found not to be in the target word by her classmates. At those times, when some of her peers laughed, she would stick out her tongue at the offender or laugh loudly also, indicating that her "mistake" had been intentional.

Mrs. Gordon did not quite know what to make of Lilian. Several months into the study, she expressed concern that Lilian might be learning-disabled and asked whether I had noticed her limitations. She wondered whether she would be better placed in special education. She mentioned that Lilian did all of her work using block letters, that she was unwilling or unable to write in cursive, and that she wrote only a sentence or two during guided composition activities.

During breaks and at lunchtime, Lilian spent her time with Marva Salas, a well-developed 14-year-old from Mexico City. Like Lilian, Marva wore bright lipstick and blue eye shadow. Often the two girls would join groups of other Latinas who, like them, appeared confident and aggressive and had little patience for the quiet, mousy girls who were trying to be good.

STARTING OUT

Soon after starting our work with the youngsters, I conducted an assessment of the focal students' English- and Spanish-language proficiencies.

The assessment was informal and involved students in reading and writing in Spanish and in speaking, reading, and writing in English. I administered the procedure to Lilian in a quiet office at the school.

Reading and Writing in Spanish

I first began by assessing Lilian's ability to read and write in Spanish. After putting her at ease about the procedure, I offered her a selection of different materials, including three or four elementary school textbooks, a magazine, and a newspaper. She was asked to choose one of the texts and to read the marked selection from it either out loud or silently. When she was finished, I asked questions about the reading. At the close of the Spanish segment of the assessment, I asked her to write about herself in Spanish.

As was typical of Lilian, she undertook the assessment tasks casually. When asked to choose a book from the materials in front of her, she turned them over quickly and looked only at the covers. She selected a third-grade textbook used in elementary schools in Mexico. She read aloud quite competently in the sing-song style typical of some rural schools, and she was able to give a short summary of what she had read, responding to specific questions with some detail.

When I asked her to write about herself in Spanish, Lilian again began the task quite casually. She wrote rapidly and produced a text which—as is typical of many young people learning to write in Spanish—contained words that were not properly segmented. The text produced by Lilian during the first assessment is laid out exactly as she wrote it. An English translation is included below it.

> SPANISH COMPOSITION, LILIAN DUQUE
> meyamo lilian nasi en Mexico
> Tengo 13 años soi buena jente mis padres
> son Mexicanos no Tengo novio megusta mucho
> ir Amisa megusta mucho la amistad Tan
> bien megusta mucho estar aqui y megusta
> mucho el Inglesh me gusta mucho estudiar
> y benir A les cuela qui siera ir Amejico
> durante 3 años y yomesienTobien se un
> poco de Inglesh me gusta estudiar de
> conputadora y Tanbien Inglesh megusta que
> men señen Abla Inglesh y yo llege Aqui
> es te año y megustomucho Aqui megusta Andaren Bike
>
> [my name is Lilian I was born in Mexico
> I am 13 I'm a nice person my parents

are Mexican I don't have a boyfriend I like
to go to mass a lot I like friendship a lot I also
like to be here and I like
English a lot I like to study a lot
and to come to school I would like to go to Mexico
for three years and I feel fine I know
a bit of English I like to study about
computer and also English I like
for them to teach me English and I got here this
year and I liked it a lot I like to ride bikes]

Lilian's composition consisted of a total of 14 unpunctuated sentences. Lilian used some sentence-initial capital letters. She also used capitals for *Mexico*, *Inglesh*, *Amejico*, and *Mexicanos*, indicating an awareness of the fact that proper names are capitalized. It is interesting to note, however, that the word *mexicanos* (like all adjectives of nationality) is not capitalized in Spanish. Other uses of capitals in the text do not seem to follow a consistent pattern.

Lilian's text is characterized by a number of word segmentation errors: (*megusta* for *me gusta*, *Amisa* for *a misa*, *meyamo* for *me llamo*, *tan bien* for *también*, *megustomucho* for *me gusta mucho*, *Andaren* for *andar en*). She also reflected Spanish-speaking students' typical confusion between *b* and *v* (*nobio* for *novio*, *benir* for *venir*), between *s*, *c*, and *z* (*nasi* for *nacir*), between *ll* and *y* (*meyamo* for *me llamo*), and between *g* and *j* (*jente* for *gente*).

Lilian's paper (examined as an informative paper following Gentile, 1992) can be considered to be a simple listing. She listed pieces of information and ideas that were all on the same topic but did not relate them well. She gave information about herself, including name, place of birth, nationality, and arrival in the United States. She also gave information about the kinds of things she liked to do. These bits of information, however, were presented out of sequence.

In spite of the many limitations in her writing, it is important to emphasize that Lilian arrived at Garden with important reading and writing abilities in Spanish. She was not illiterate, and she did not appear to be "slow." She had a good notion of what texts were and how to read them as well as a clear sense of what writing involved. She had basic L1 academic skills upon which to build as she acquired English.

Beginning English-Language Abilities

As compared to her Spanish abilities, Lilian's English was almost nonexistent. In assessing Lilian's English I used specially prepared tasks and procedures. I began with a series of personal information questions that required her to respond to inquiries about name, address, place of birth, previous schooling, family composition, and daily routine to which Lilian valiantly attempted to respond. Seeing her clear limitations, I skipped the second part of the assessment, which involved brief role-playing situations (buying something, making a long-distance phone call, going to the emergency room). I moved on to the third part of the assessment, which focused on her ability to use English for academic purposes (e.g., reading text materials and writing).

Lilian knew a few words of English—*dog, cat, ice cream*—but it was apparent that she understood very little. Examples of Lilian's responses to the first segment of the language assessment, focusing on her ability to provide personal information, is included below.

As will be noted, Lilian was able to understand and respond to my first two questions quite well.

Interviewer: What is your name?
Lilian: My name is Lilian Duque.   *(Understands/responds)*
Interviewer: Oh, Lilian Duque? How are
   you Lilian?
Lilian: Fine.   *(Understands/responds)*

In most cases, however, Lilian was unable to respond in English. She indicated her comprehension of what was asked by translating the question or by responding to the question in Spanish.

Interviewer: You're fine, good. Where do
   you live?
Lilian: Dónde vivo?   *(Translates question)*
Interviewer: mmm
Lilian: Ladera   *(Gives street name)*

In a number of cases, Lilian failed to understand very simple questions.

Interviewer: OK. How old are you?
Lilian: um   *(Fails to understand)*
Interviewer: What is your age? Are you 11,
   12? 13?
Lilian: Oh, trece años.   *(Responds after rephrasing
                                                of question/uses hint pro-
                                                vided)*

Lilian was also unable to respond to questions concerning her favorite activities and her favorite foods. She had an equally difficult time in talking about her family in English.

Reading and Writing in English

In order to assess Lilian's reading abilities in English, I offered her a colorful youth magazine that had many pictures and illustrations along with articles on a number of different subjects (e.g., circuses, plants, animals) that I thought would be familiar to youngsters who had just arrived in this country. I asked her to leaf through the magazine and to find something that interested her. I requested that she "read" an article and then tell me something about what she had read.

The purpose of this task was to determine Lilian's ability to transfer knowledge that she had acquired from reading in Spanish to reading in English. I wanted to see if she would be able to "read" illustrations, use cognates, and draw on prior knowledge to carry out the task. As expected, Lilian did indeed try to apply her word-attack skills in Spanish in order to read in English, but she gave up when the words made no sense. When instructed to do so, however, Lilian was also able to hypothesize about what different articles in the magazine were about. When I taught her how to do so, she was also able to hypothesize about larger text meaning based on key familiar words in section headings and on the illustrations in the article.

When Lilian had completed the reading task, I asked her to write in English. I did not suggest a topic but simply said that she could write whatever she wanted. Lilian's initial attempt to write in English was very basic. Her entire text is include below.

> Hi! Bak Telephone Namer
> Door wvindow Dor clak boy bebe
> haus cap map

As will be noted, Lilian's text is a simple listing of isolated words. Some words are correctly spelled and other words (e.g., *clak, haus*) have been written according to Spanish spelling conventions. In comparison to her writing in Spanish, Lilian could not yet write a single sentence in English.

At the time that the study began, Lilian had been in the United States a little over 2 months. She was slowly beginning to understand English phrases used in everyday interaction. She had had no experience, however, in attempting to use English outside of the school setting.

Low as her Spanish reading and writing abilities might seem to be, they were nevertheless developed to some degree. Lilian could write a connected text, and she could draw meaning from written text. During the assessment, she was willing to approach English reading from a top-down perspective and to attempt to use illustrations, headings, and so on to conjecture about meaning.

ACCESS TO ENGLISH AT SCHOOL

As might be expected from my description of the NEP core course at Garden, Lilian—although enrolled in an English-only school and program—had very limited access to authentic English-language use within the school setting. During the seventh-grade year spent at Garden School, for example, Lilian had the schedule shown in Table 4.1. She spent the first three periods of the day in Mrs. Gordon's classroom and the fourth period outdoors in PE. She spent the final three periods in subject-matter classes especially designed for non-English-speaking students.

During the NEP core, Lilian had very restricted access to English. Most classroom activities were repetitive (e.g., punctuation correction, hang-the-spider), offering neither large amounts of comprehensible input nor opportunities for engaging in negotiated interactions. Mrs. Gordon's curriculum did not include teaching students expressions needed in order to get personal needs met; to express needs, feelings, or ideas; or to share and request information. At best, the NEP core offered Lilian samples of connected

Table 4.1. Lilian's Schedule

Period	Classes
1	NEP core
2	NEP core
3	NEP core
4	PE
5	NEP sheltered science
6	NEP sheltered math
7	NEP sheltered computers

discourse (the reading of the monkey stories) that she could not understand, samples of academic explanations that she could ignore and still complete the assignment, worksheets in which she filled in single English words, sentences to copy from the board, and drill and practice exercises on single vocabulary items. Homework involved writing different sets of words (e.g., numbers from 1 to 50) that students were expected to spell correctly.

During the course of the schoolday Lilian had no direct access to English-speaking peers except during PE, where half of the students were mainstream, English-speaking students. However, the two groups did not interact with each other. Activities seem to involve lining up to shoot baskets and running around the field. The teacher did not seem to attempt to organize activities in order to bring the groups of students together in any way.

SHELTERED CLASSES

Lilian's sheltered classes also offered her very restricted access to English. As will be recalled, at Garden Middle School sheltered instruction was implemented with students like Lilian who were at almost zero English. The guidelines indicating that such instruction be used only with students at the intermediate (LEP) level were simply disregarded. The task of actually teaching subject matter to students who did not understand any English at all, however, was challenging indeed. Interviews with teachers revealed that they spent hours preparing presentations with accompanying visuals in order to get across only one or two main concepts.

Lilian was enrolled in Mrs. Jackson's afternoon sheltered math class, in Mrs. Emerson's sheltered science course, and in Mrs. Thompson's sheltered computer class. Each of these classes enrolled only NEP and LEP students, many of whom were also in Mrs. Gordon's NEP core. Each of these classes, in spite of the teachers' often valiant efforts, provided very limited access to subject-matter content. They also provided very restricted access to English as well. The limitations of the sheltered approach can perhaps be best illustrated by describing Lilian's sheltered science class.

For sheltered science, Lilian was enrolled in Mrs. Emerson's class. Mrs. Emerson was an extraordinarily creative teacher who had the reputation of running her science classes in such a way that her mainstream students were busy every moment. She pushed students to enter the science fair, she arranged frequent field trips, and she had a strong hands-on approach to teaching concepts. For her regular classes, she designed activities that required group interaction, individual time management in carrying out sets of activities, and much freedom to explore and question.

With her NEP science class, Mrs. Emerson experienced many frustrations. She found it difficult to explain even the most mundane kinds of things, such as how to fold and cut paper to make a particular project. It was impossible to move through activities quickly, to group students, and to have them move efficiently from task to task. Most of her energy was taken up with trivial matters rather than with teaching subject-matter concepts.

Mrs. Emerson tried many things to engage the NEP students. During the fall semester, for example, in order to excite students about the study of outer space, she sponsored a contest for her mainstream classes that involved making posters of the entire life cycle of stars. Much time and attention was given by the regular mainstream students to researching this life cycle and to creating illustrations and texts to reflect the complexity of the process. On the day in which the charts and posters were finished, Mrs. Emerson looked forward eagerly to having the NEP group vote on the best poster. She imagined that they would learn something from looking at the posters and that they would feel a part of the science community at Garden School.

The NEP students sat quietly at black-surfaced tables, four to a table. Some looked up curiously at the star charts, which were 8 feet long and hung up around the room. Others giggled and chatted quietly. Mrs. Emerson moved to the front of the room and began to pass out bags of crayons and sheets of paper. She motioned to the star charts and explained that she wanted students to tear off a piece of the paper and write down the number of their favorite chart. Students looked up but did not move. Impatient, Mrs. Emerson took a piece of paper from her own desk, tore off a corner, and wrote a number. "You have to vote," she insisted. "Just tear off a piece of paper, write a number, and pass it up here."

One or two students began to move. They folded the paper slowly, creasing it, preparing to cut off a piece neatly. Others students looked around and began to copy their peers' behavior. Some whispered in Spanish, asking their tablemates what number they should write down. No one appeared to be interested in looking at the star charts.

Ten minutes into the period, Mrs. Emerson sighed in frustration and began the day's activity. She passed out a worksheet containing a number of blanks and moved to the overhead projector. The worksheet had the following text. All italicized words were blank in the original.

The *force of gravity* holds the rockets and the *astronauts down* on the planet earth.

The *action* of the burning *gases* causes the reaction of the rocket *lifting*.

First the *rocket orbits* or circles the planet *earth*.

Then it moves to the *moon* on its own *power* because an object in *motion* wants to *stay* in motion.

Working rapidly, Mrs. Emerson used the overhead to fill in blanks in a sample worksheet. As she filled in each blank, she talked about the concept. For example, she reached for a large globe and spun a pencil around it to suggest what the word *orbit* meant. She repeated, exaggerated, and used a variety of objects to convey concepts of lifting, gravity, and so on. It was not clear how well the students understood these concepts. The teacher did not ask questions to determine what was understood, nor did any of the kids ask questions.

The activity then moved to the making of posters to illustrate the concepts summarized on the worksheet. This complicated activity involved folding poster paper in a particular way, making lines with rulers that were passed out, cutting out the filled-in worksheets to paste on the poster paper (scissors were also passed out), and finally drawing figures of a rocket. Kids were told that this was exciting because they were getting to color using a special silver crayon.

I helped in carrying out the activity and passed out scissors and rulers. Much had to be accomplished in 44 minutes. Most of the students were confused. Mrs. Emerson moved from one table to another, pantomiming, holding up her own completed model of the rocket poster. During the course of the class I was aware that Mrs. Emerson was trying desperately to use the classroom procedures that had been successful with her mainstream students. She wanted students to be engaged, to work in groups, and to produce something they could see. She was a good teacher who loved science and wanted to communicate her excitement to both her mainstream and her NEP students. However, as a monolingual, English-speaking teacher who did not even have a Spanish-speaking instructional aide in the room, she was at an extraordinary disadvantage. In the sheltered classroom, even the most trivial instructions were not grasped. Youngsters misunderstood what to do, skipped over steps, confused their tablemates, and often ended up quite frustrated themselves. In the case of the rocket poster activity, for example, what Mrs. Emerson spent most of her time focusing on was the folding of the paper, the drawing of the lines on the paper, the cutting and pasting of the filled-in worksheets, and finally the coloring of the rocket itself.

Lilian carried out the activity in her usual manner. She waited until others were working and then began to work. Thinking she had figured out what to do, she folded the paper the wrong way. Confused, she looked up again, careful to put forward her very bored I-don't-care look. At the end of the period, she had produced a sloppy version of the poster in which she had pulled off and repasted the worksheet.

In terms of access to English, the sheltered science class—like the sheltered math and the sheltered computer classes—gave Lilian access to segments of connected English that were often illustrated by pictures, drawings, and pantomimed explanations. She understood little, however, about the concepts being explained. Moreover, she had very few opportunities to develop her productive abilities in English. She did not need to speak in these classes either to respond to or to ask questions. Nor was she asked to attempt to read text materials in English. The class texts, which had colorful illustrations of stars, planets, and rockets, were not used with the NEP students because it was assumed that they could not read English.

To make it through the day in her sheltered content classes, Lilian developed several key strategies. She pretended to listen, and, when called up to complete some task in class, she would quickly imitate her classmates' behavior. If it ever became evident to either her peers or her teacher that she had not understood or that she had done an assignment incorrectly, Lilian would quickly pretend not to care.

JOINING A GANG

There was much concern in the city of Mission Vista and at Garden School about gangs and gang activity. School personnel met frequently with local law enforcement officers to work together on what was considered a growing problem. As was the case in other areas of California, two gangs had been identified in the area: the *Norteños* and the *Sureños*. Both gangs were made up exclusively of Latino youngsters. The *Sureños* generally attracted newly arrived youngsters and was considered to be the fastest-growing gang. The *Norteños*, on the other hand, attracted more "assimilated" Latinos, that is, Latinos who had been born in the country, who were primarily identified with the United States, and who had become or were increasingly becoming English-speaking. Law enforcement personnel were particularly worried about the influence of "colors," that is, about nice kids aligning themselves with one group or the other. They were also worried about full-fledged gang members coming to the community from the Los Angeles area.

From the assistant principal I learned that there were very few known gang members at Garden. There were, however, a number of students whose older siblings were thought to be involved in gang activities and who seemed to fit the pattern of gang wannabes. School personnel kept a close watch on such youngsters, and community liaison personnel (e.g., the migrant education liaison, school counselors) tapped as many sources of information as they could in order to anticipate possible problems.

At meetings, police officers generally told parents to be vigilant for gang-related paraphernalia, that is, for gang symbols drawn on arms or hands to suggest tattoos, use of stylized gang symbols to decorate book covers and notebooks, use of particular hand gestures, wearing of particular colors, and frequent fights with other students. It was generally thought that gang activity in Mission Vista was the most common on Ladera Street. Students who lived in apartments in this area were considered to be particularly at risk.

By October of her first year in the United States, Lilian's life was directly touched by gang warfare. Her older brother was shot in the shoulder. According to newspaper reports, a fight had broken out between members of the two rival gangs. Several gang members pulled out knives. Shots rang out as the police arrived. Gang members ran as Lilian's brother Sergio fell to the ground.

When Lilian mentioned the incident and identified the injured young man as her brother, I admit that I was somewhat taken aback. I remembered reading about the shooting in the paper, but I had never imagined how very close it was to the lives of students I knew. Lilian talked about what had happened matter-of-factly, saying that Sergio was simply defending his friends. She also said that her mother had been very frightened and that Sergio would have to go to a special school. She did not specifically mention gangs. According to the migrant education liaison who worked closely with the Latino immigrant students, however, Lilian was very much at risk. She now had a 19-year-old boyfriend who was a *Sureño* (a member of the *Sureños* gang) and a friend of her brother's.

According to Mrs. Duque, Lilian was constantly involved in fights with other girls. She recounted her advice to Lilian (for which I have provided a translation) as follows:

> Yo le digo que no se pelié, que se ponga otros colores.
> I tell her not to fight, to wear other colors.

From her remarks, I suspected that Mrs. Duque had some idea of the fact that certain colors were a problem. It did not appear, however, that she clearly understood how seriously gangs were taken by both school personnel and law enforcement officers in Mission Vista.

In May, Lilian talked about being a member of a gang after a language assessment interview. She said she was *Sureña* and explained that her group was different from the *Norteños*. She was vague about the difference between the two gangs, but she pointed out that *Sureña* girls could not go out with *Norteño* guys. *Norteños* spoke English, she informed us. *Sureños* did not. What is perhaps most interesting about the conversation is that Lilian did not seem reluctant to respond to my questions about what had been required to become a member of the *Sureños*. She described being beaten by a group of girls, taking it, and then fighting back.

I brought up the subject of gangs on other occasions when I thought that Lilian would not become alarmed by my questions. I learned little more than she had told me before. When she spoke about being in the gang, it was always in reference to guys in her neighborhood that she liked or did not like. Once when she walked me to my car after I had visited her family, she pointed out that she could not be interested in an attractive young man who cordially greeted her because he was a *Norteño*. *Sureño* guys had to have *Sureña* girlfriends, and vice versa. She confided that most of her fights—including those that she had in school—had to do with guys. Other girls were always accusing her of flirting with their boyfriends and of trying to steal them away. She was not about to tolerate anyone calling her a *puta* (whore).

For Garden Middle School administrators, Lilian quickly became identified as a behavior problem. She flirted constantly with the young men in her classes and appeared to enjoy provoking the wrath of the offended girlfriend of whatever young man she directed her attention at. She engaged in noisy verbal fights during breaks and during the lunch hour and sometimes returned to class showing signs of having engaged in physical fighting as well. On one occasion, in the middle of Mrs. Davidson's class, Lilian started a fight then and there. She got up from her desk, shouted insults at another girl, and reached out to pull her hair. The other girl landed a blow on Lilian's face. Raising her voice and moving to pull the girls apart, Mrs. Davidson focused her attention on Lilian, grabbing her by the arm, pushing her toward the door, and walking her toward the principal's office. When I saw Lilian later, she was seething in anger and could not understand why the other girl, who had hit her, had not been sent to the office as well.

ENGLISH AT THE END OF THE FIRST YEAR

Many things happened to Lilian in her first year. She entered a new world, and she found a way to survive. Her survival, however, had little to do with doing well in school or with learning English. She focused her energies on being one of the most attractive Latina girls in the school and on becoming strong and aggressive and nobody's fool. Her abilities in English improved only slightly between November and May. During the second assessment, she was still not able to engage in an interaction in which she was asked for personal information. She could understand many of the questions asked but still could not respond in English. I had no doubt that the following year Lilian would again be placed in the NEP core.

THE SECOND YEAR: THE ESL PROGRAM AT CRENSHAW SCHOOL

During the summer, the Duque family, at the insistence of a social worker who was following Sergio's case, moved away from Ladera Street to another area of Mission Vista. As a result, Lilian transferred to Crenshaw School, which was part of a different school district and served a section of the city in which few recent immigrants had taken up residence. The school itself sits on a quiet street among modest tract houses. During the period of the study, it was in good repair and freshly painted gray. The playing fields behind it were grassy and well tended.

During that year, there were few ESL students at Crenshaw. As opposed to Garden Middle School, where the population of newly arrived Latino students was growing and where two teachers taught three different levels of ESL, there was a single newcomer classroom at Crenshaw. All non-English-speaking or limited-English-speaking students in the school who were enrolled in grades 5 through 8 (about 25 students) were placed in the newcomer classroom. Therefore Lilian, who was a well-developed eighth-grader, was placed in the same classroom with very small fifth-graders who still behaved and looked like little children.

In general, newcomer programs such as the one at Crenshaw have as their goal providing students with a safe environment in which they can learn English. It is expected that students placed in such programs will move quickly into regular placements after a period of intensive English-language instruction. At Crenshaw School, however, mainstreaming did not take place as quickly as the school might have wished. We were told that ordinarily Asian students who came into the newcomer program stayed only 1 year before being placed in regular mainstream classes. Latino students, on the other hand, generally stayed in the newcomer class for 2 or even 3 years. Some students never officially exited from the class; they moved from Crenshaw to beginning ESL programs at the high school level.

The teacher in charge of the newcomer class at Crenshaw during the second year of the study was Griselda Sikorsky, a woman of Polish background who had herself been an ESL student in this country. A husky, tall, and powerful woman, Mrs. Sikorsky appeared to be deeply committed to her students and to providing a safe and pleasant environment. She was assisted by a teacher's aide, Mrs. Monique Paheau, a Peruvian woman of French extraction. During the year that Lilian was at Crenshaw, there were 25 students in the newcomer classroom.

The daily class schedule and curriculum areas are shown in Table 4.2. Each day began with the lowest-ability students working with Mrs. Paheau on spelling and then on language and reading. This group sat in Mrs. Paheau's teaching area, where they generally worked with sentences and words. The list of vocabulary words were written on Mrs. Paheau's board, and students were asked to make up sentences using these particular words. Each sentence volunteered by students was written on the board with appropriate modifications and corrections. For example, when a child volunteered the sentence "The moon is the color yellow," Mrs. Paheau modified it and wrote, "The moon is yellow."

Sentences generated during these activities included:

The sandwich is for lunch.
The seven is little.
The dog is yellow and orange.
The seal is black.
The seesaw goes up and down.

From time to time, Mrs. Paheau would use Spanish to clarify a particular meaning or concept. She did so even though two students in the group were Vietnamese. Once all sentences were written on the board, students copied the sentences into their notebooks.

During the first and second period, the second-lowest-ability group worked with Mrs. Sikorsky in her teaching area on both spelling and language/reading. Students in the highest-ability group remained at their desks working on other activities until it was their turn to work with Mrs. Sikorsky.

Table 4.2. Newcomer Class Daily Schedule

Period	Curriculum Area
1	Spelling
2	Language/reading
3	PE
4	Math
5	Math tutoring
6	Crafts
7	Crafts

During the time devoted to spelling, Mrs. Sikorsky, like Mrs. Paheau, elicited sentences from her students. These sentences were also based on a list of words placed prominently on the front board. On one occasion, for example, this list included *hold*, *only*, *even*, *me*, *we*, *open*, *both*, and *before*. The sentences generated by the students and written by Mrs. Sikorsky on the board were simple sentences such as the following:

Lilian has only one dollar.
I don't even have a penny.
My dad is with me.

The Teaching of Reading

The teaching of reading in the newcomer classroom centered around a set of elementary basal readers. Students in the middle group, the group in which Lilian was placed, were reading a second-grade basal. The group to be instructed sat in the appropriate teaching area. The teacher—either Mrs. Sikorsky or Mrs. Paheau—called on students to read aloud from the class text while the other students followed along. Occasionally the teacher would read aloud for a few minutes.

When listening to students read, Mrs. Sikorsky generally focused on the meaning of the story, correcting only blatant errors in pronunciation. Because the elementary school readers were somewhat infantile for adolescent students, however, the teachers had to struggle to keep students focused on the stories recounting the escapades of little bears and other such creatures. She would stop at key points in the story, asking students to recall a particular event or detail in the story.

Such reading instruction assumed that ESL students needed to learn how to read in English by reading texts intended for young readers. Except for the high-ability group, students in the newcomer class did not read any materials that in any way resembled the kinds of texts they might encounter in regular mainstream classes. Like the students at Garden School, students in the ESL or newcomer program at Crenshaw received no instruction in reading for gist, guessing details from context, skimming, scanning, and so on.

The Teaching of Writing

Instruction in writing was also very limited. Students copied sentences from the board, filled in blanks in sentences, and copied long lists of words in English that they then translated into Spanish. The only activity observed during the entire schoolyear involving even controlled writing involved responding to a list of questions about the reading, for which students composed answers. The teacher was careful to provide models, such as that presented in Figure 4.1, of what student papers should look like. The teacher also provided a model form for students' answers:

Buzzy Bear saw ——————.

She also provided hints to help them remember to use the appropriate verb tense:

Today I see, yesterday I saw.

It is interesting to note that everything written on the board was written in block letters. Neither of the two teachers used cursive.

The Teaching of Other Subject Matter

In the newcomer classroom, students did not have access to the regular curriculum. They did not, for example, have a class in science or in social studies. They did, however, receive individualized math instruction from both Mrs. Sikorsky and Mrs. Paheau. During the two periods of the day designated as math and math tutorial, students sat at their desks and worked on math at the level that had been found to be appropriate for them. One student, then, might be working on times tables while another was working on converting fractions to lowest terms. Students used different texts or were on different pages of the same text. Teachers circulated among the students and responded to questions as students needed help. The advantage of using this method for teaching mathematics was that

Figure 4.1. A Model of a Student Paper

Name   Reading

Date   Period 2

(skip a line)

Buzzy Bear and the Rainbow

1. What did Buzzy Bear see in the sky?

Latino students whose English was still quite weak could receive instruction and explanations in Spanish from Mrs. Paheau. Since explanations were tailored to their questions, students could work at their appropriate math level.

Getting into Trouble

As was the case at Garden during the latter part of the year, Lilian became a behavior problem at Crenshaw School. She continued to fight with other girls, to flirt with all the young men in the class, and to make little effort to study and to keep up with assignments. What was different at Crenshaw was that, because Mrs. Paheau spoke Spanish, Lilian could get away with a great deal less than she had at Garden. On several occasions, Mrs. Paheau had taken it upon herself to call Mrs. Duque to inform her that Lilian was falling behind or that she was fighting and getting into trouble. It appeared that, at times, Lilian enjoyed the attention she received from Mrs. Paheau. At other times, she viewed Mrs. Paheau as her enemy.

There was no question, however, that Lilian was on the verge of becoming involved in serious trouble. One incident, which took place in January of the year she spent at Crenshaw, can best illustrate how Lilian behaved, what she communicated about her feelings, and how others responded to her.

During the second semester, I arrived at Crenshaw one afternoon at about 1:30 P.M. When I went to the main office and proceeded to sign in as a school visitor, I noticed Lilian sitting there. She was wearing blue jeans, a royal-blue sweatshirt, and laced-up black suede shoes. When I laughingly asked if she was in trouble, she responded that she was going to be suspended because she had been in a fight with another girl (a Salvadorean). She said that the fight with the girl started because the Salvadorean girl was now going with Lilian's former boyfriend, Roberto. The girl had been trying to make her jealous and had called her a *puta*.

In talking about the fight, Lilian claimed that Mrs. Paheau had taken the other girl's side. Lilian felt strongly that Mrs. Paheau did not like her. She had no idea for how long a period she was going to be suspended. She did say, however, that if the other girl was not suspended also, she did not plan to return to school.

Hoping to be of help, I told Lilian to wait for me in the office and that I would talk to Mrs. Sikorsky and Mrs. Paheau. I was aware that there was trouble in the Duque household. In fact, Lilian had called me twice during the past week to ask whether I knew if she could get a job. Her father was in jail for driving while intoxicated. Because he was a repeat offender, he would be in jail for 4 months. Lilian was worried about the rent and had said that neither her older brother nor sister was working.

I went to the classroom—fortunately the other students were out at PE. I gathered that the fight had been very serious indeed. I listened, explained my concerns about the family, and asked for permission to take Lilian home.

As we walked to find Lilian, Mrs. Paheau commented that Lilian had convinced herself that Mrs. Paheau disliked the Mexican students. She complained that Lilian did no homework, used bad language constantly, and made things difficult for her best friend, Adela. Mrs. Paheau was worried about her safety because of gang activity and said that Adela had been found holding a gun that she claimed belonged to Lilian. She also said that Lilian had been seen by other students bringing beer to school and drinking behind the building in the morning.

When we arrived at the Duque family's apartment, Lilian commented that the house was *un mugrero* (a mess), and indeed it was. In the living room were a wooden dining room table, a sofa, a cot, and three chairs lined up as though someone had slept across all three the night before. Across from the door was a bedroom in which there were two sets of bunk beds. The whole house was very untidy: dirty dishes in the sink; the smell of stale food; counters full of dishes, pots, pans, both dirty and clean; package wrappings casually tossed on the floor. Lilian closed the bedroom door, and we sat down to talk.

I lectured her about her behavior at school and about the importance of getting an education. Lilian's focus was not on what had happened at school, however. She told me that she hated her father's drinking and the fighting between her mother and her father. Her uncle (her father's brother) who lived with them drank heavily also. Sometimes both men would drink together and her uncle would say ugly things about Lilian's mother. Lilian disclosed tearfully that she had thought about leaving the house and just going somewhere else. She did not know where or with whom.

My feelings on leaving Lilian that afternoon were ones of sadness and despair. I could talk about the importance of doing well in school and of learning English, but it would have little impact on Lilian's life, on what really mattered to her, and on what really hurt her on a day-to-day basis.

Later on that same evening, I talked with Mrs. Duque on the phone. She quickly told me that the school had called to tell her about Lilian's fight and that she had reprimanded Lilian. I have included the English translation of what we said.

Le acabo de pegar y ay se salió. Le dije que le voy a quemar toda la ropa azul. Dice mis Paheau que es muy grosera con ella. Yo le digo que con todos los problemas que tengo y luego esto. No está bien.

[I just hit her and she left. I told her that I'm gong to burn all her blue clothes. Mrs. Paheau says that she is very rude to her. I tell her that with all the problems I've got and then this. It isn't right.]

Mrs. Duque felt strongly that Lilian needed to go to school, to do her work, and to avoid trouble. She appreciated hearing from Mrs. Paheau, but she was not altogether sure that Mrs. Paheau knew what was going on in Lilian's life. She said firmly:

Yo soy muy estricta con ellas. No es cierto, que Lilian ande con los cholos allá de la calle Ladera. Lilian llega a la casa y no sale.

[I'm very strict with them. It's not true that Lilian is going with the *cholos* (guys/gang types) from Ladera Street. Lilian gets home and she doesn't go out.]

Mrs. Duque also spoke about her husband and his problems. He was scheduled to be in court the next day, and Mrs. Duque was hoping that he would be sentenced to highway cleanup on weekends so that he would able to work at his everyday job. She had desperately been trying to get an appointment with someone in the social services department to see if any help was available for the family. In the meantime, she had sent her older daughter to work in her place cleaning houses.

She explained that her husband had been drunk, had hit two cars, and had left the scene of the accident. The insurance companies were suing Mrs. Duque's boss, the person who had sold them the truck that her husband had been driving. Additionally, moreover, the family who rented out a room in their apartment for $200 had moved out. She was not sure how they would eat and pay the rent.

Progress Made by Lilian at Crenshaw

As might be expected given the tensions in Lilian's life, Lilian made little progress in terms of her English-language proficiency. Her lack of progress, however, was not entirely her fault. As had been the case at Garden, Lilian had very limited access to English during the schoolday. In the newcomer classroom, most student-to-student interaction took place in Spanish. The presence of the Spanish-speaking aide, while greatly beneficial to students in many respects, also resulted in students hearing less English in the class-room—especially during the two math periods when they called on Mrs. Paheau to explain or clarify particularly difficult concepts.

Lilian progressed little in her productive abilities in English. At the end of the study, she spoke a very limited amount of English and had been unable to move beyond a very low level in writing English. In terms of receptive skills, however, her listening comprehension abilities seemed to have improved greatly. Her reading abilities, on the other hand, reflected the limits of the instruction she had received both at Garden School and in the newcomer program at Crenshaw.

LILIAN AFTER 2 YEARS

Two years after arriving in the United States, Lilian had changed a great deal. The village child who first wrote about being happy and about want-ing to learn English had turned into an angry and rebellious young adoles-cent. Both within her family and at school, she struggled to assert herself. She wanted desperately to be strong.

Neither Garden nor Crenshaw schools were equipped to deal with the many problems in Lilian's life. There was little at school that genuinely interested her. Moreover, neither she nor her family really understood why doing well in school was important for her future. Still, it is impossible not to wonder what might have happened to Lilian if Garden Middle School had been different. What if school had been interesting? What if classroom activities had been engaging and challenging? What if she had been able to develop a school identity that was not oppositional in order to survive?

5

Elisa

Twelve-year-old Elisa was small and dark-complected, with high cheekbones and very straight black hair. When school began, Elisa and her sister Elvia (then 11) had been in the United States for only a few weeks. They were from a small village in Honduras. Their mother, Magda, who had been in this country for more than 8 years, had finally been able to send for the two daughters.

Elisa was homesick. She missed her grandmother, her school, and the places that they went to near the small town where they lived. Like many other newly arrived children, Elisa was not aware that she was an emergent teen. In Honduras, she was considered a child by her grandmother, the rest of the family, and the teachers at school.

Elisa spoke of her old school fondly. She missed the rhythm of the schoolday: going home at noon, having lunch, returning at 2:00 P.M. for the afternoon session, and finally going home after school at 5:00. In her new American school, the days seemed incredibly short. When school ended, both Elisa and her sister slowly walked home, where they would spend the rest of the afternoon and evening alone. Their mother, who worked a late-night shift, would not return until both the children had gone to sleep. Both girls were very lonely, and often days would pass before they really saw their mother.

The family lived in a two-bedroom apartment in a four-unit apartment complex. Magda and her girls rented out the second bedroom to a young man who was newly arrived and who had no family in the area. He was given limited kitchen privileges and was generally not at home when the girls arrived after school.

Magda had initially traveled from Honduras to the New York area sponsored by her father, who was a naturalized American citizen. When she moved to Los Angeles 2 years later, she could make herself understood in English very well. Six years later, when we began our study, Magda could carry out a wide variety of interactions in flawed but very functional

English. She was determined that her daughters would learn to speak the language well and that they would not have heavy Spanish accents.

As a single parent with no training and a great deal of responsibility, Magda needed to work at several jobs. Once her daughters arrived, the pressures on her became enormous. She worked the late shift in a factory, took care of a sick old man at night and on weekends, and cleaned houses most weekend mornings. Often she would leave before the children woke up and return long after they had gone to sleep.

The children lived their lives according to very strict rules. They went home immediately after school; they could not have friends over, nor could they go outside at all. They could sit in their apartment, watch television, and do their homework. Magda called the girls from work whenever she had a free moment.

Magda was well known at school. From one of her employers, Magda learned that it was important for parents to go to school often, to meet the girls' teachers, and to attend all open houses and special meetings. Many teachers at Garden Middle School had met Magda and were quite impressed with her. The fact that she spoke English and that she volunteered occasionally in one class or another made her very different from other Latina immigrant mothers. One teacher was most impressed with Magda and believed that she was a very educated woman who worked in the computer industry.

The fact is that Magda tried as hard as she could to get every piece of information that could help her children. When we met, she quickly deluged me with questions. It was obvious that she knew little about what the ESL program was, what sheltered classes were, and how her children were doing. I explained the difference between mainstream instruction and her daughter's placement to Magda several times and shared with her details about how Elisa was doing in class. It was not easy, however, for Magda to understand the subtle labels of the classes that designated very different school realities.

Like many other immigrants, Magda understood only enough to get by most of the time. There were many things, however, that she did not understand. For example, she was offered a job as a teachers' aide in a neighboring elementary school by school personnel who had been impressed by seeing her at Garden. She took the job five mornings a week and soon found out that to keep the job she would need to get her G.E.D. She did not know what a G.E.D. was, but she smiled during the interview and said that indeed she had begun to take community college classes and would soon get her G.E.D. It took me many hours to explain how high schools work in this country, what a high school diploma is, and how someone can work on a G.E.D. When she finally understood, she seemed quite sure that she could do well on whatever test was required. She felt that her only problem was writing in English—writing defined as spelling and vocabulary.

As it turned out, Magda worked as a teachers' aide for only a few months. It became evident to the teachers that she lacked many essential skills and abilities in both academic English and Spanish and that she had trouble helping the children with even beginning reading and writing. Magda was somewhat upset but determined to move forward. By then, she had bought a G.E.D. book and had begun attending the self-paced program at the local adult education center. Soon, however, she felt overwhelmed and could barely make it through a page or two at a time. She felt embarrassed that Elisa appeared to know much more than she did. Telling herself and all of us that she would return after she took some more ESL classes, she dropped out of the program and enrolled in an ESL grammar class at a local community college. Several weeks into the quarter, Magda had dropped out again. The teacher found much fault with her spoken English, and Magda could make little sense of the principal parts of the English verbs.

IN THE CLASSROOM

In the classroom, Elisa was quiet and well behaved. She worked carefully and deliberately no matter how trivial the assignment. When asked a question by one of her tablemates, she responded politely and quickly returned to her work. Even when the entire class became noisy, Elisa sat at her seat writing, copying, or coloring. Mrs. Gordon consistently sat Federico, the suspected gang wannabe, next to Elisa because she would not be distracted easily. With Federico, as well as with most of her other classmates, Elisa kept a cordial distance.

Typically, Elisa was concerned about doing things correctly. Early in the first year, she took great pains in coloring the small illustrations on every one of her vocabulary worksheets. Where other students clearly recognized the task as busywork, Elisa approached it as important. She selected crayons thoughtfully, picking one up, putting it down, and selecting another. Finally, having found the perfect color, she filled in a part of the illustration.

Whenever Mrs. Gordon spoke, Elisa looked up and appeared to be listening carefully. Even though during the entire first year she did not raise her hand to volunteer to correct punctuation exercises or to suggest letters for hang-the-spider, she could respond if called upon to do so. During the reading of the monkey books by Mrs. Gordon, Elisa usually began by sitting on one leg in an effort to get a better view of the book being held up at the front of the room. After a few minutes, it became evident that her attention had wandered. She looked down at her desk, fidgeted, and occasionally looked up. From time to time, she sneaked a glance at the classroom clock.

During the first year, Elisa was also eager to copy whatever Mrs. Gordon put on the board. She followed the guided composition exercises to the letter and seldom attempted to create her own sentences. She studied for every test (e.g., spelling of the days of the week, spelling of cardinal numbers) and was delighted when she did well. She seemed eager to do more work, to write down more lists, to copy more words from books, and to keep busy.

Surprisingly, Elisa did not particularly impress her teacher. Mrs. Gordon appeared to take Elisa for granted. She arrived on time, she behaved, and she demanded little attention. In Mrs. Gordon's class, however, being good may actually have worked against Elisa. Over the course of the schoolyear, the teacher had little sense of how Elisa's English-language abilities were developing. Close attention to English development was reserved for the Asian children whose parents regularly requested more homework, a quick transition to advanced LEP and mainstream classes, and clear signs of progress. Even though Mrs. Gordon consistently complained about the Asian parents and their "pushiness," she responded to their requests and both provided and corrected more assignments for their children. Elisa's mother, on the other hand, was not pushy.

STARTING OUT

As with Lilian, early in the fall of the first year I conducted an assessment of Elisa's English- and Spanish-language proficiencies. I administered the procedure to Elisa in the same quiet office where I had assessed Lilian.

Reading and Writing in Spanish

For the Spanish reading segment of the assessment, Elisa chose a sixth-grade science book used in the United States in bilingual education programs. She leafed through it and then began to read aloud. She read smoothly and confidently and was able to summarize what she had read.

Elisa's writing abilities appeared to be much the same as Lilian's. In Honduras, writing had been used primarily for copying assignments, for copying texts, and perhaps for taking dictation. Original composing was very rarely done.

In response to our request that she write about herself under the general title *Yo*, Elisa produced the following text, which is laid out exactly as she wrote it, including crossed-out words.

CONPOSICIÓN A ELISA LARA
Yo soy Elisa Lara soy muy buena para cocinar
y mi abi favorito es cantar soy trigueña de pelo negro y
indio soy de ojos cafe oscuros y tengo 12
años cuando este grande me gustaria peinar y pintar
a las artistas yo respeto a mi mamá y a toda, mi
familia Mi abuelita me enseño a respetar y amar a
mi familia y me gusta ~~de y me~~ respetarlos
heso es muy bueno niños que no respetan a sus
padres ~~no ses lo respeta a~~ es que no se le a
respetado a el yo respetó porque me respetan
Yo soy Elisa Lara y me gusta ~~de~~ el ingles
y yo voy a aprender ingles para poderme superar
en esté paiz.

COMPOSITION TO ELISA LARA
[I am Elisa Lara I am very good at
cooking and my favorite hobby is
singing I'm dark-skinned with black
and Indian hair I have dark brown
eyes and I am twelve years old when I
grow up I would like to comb and
paint actresses I respect my mother
and all, my family My grandmother
taught me to respect and love my
family and I like to respect them that
is very good children that don't
respect their parents is that he has
not been respected I respect because I
am respected I am Elisa Lara and I
like English and I am going to learn
English so I can get ahead in this
country]

In writing a personal description of herself, Elisa wrote a total of 12 sentences. In terms of form, Elisa's writing reflected minimal attention to capitalization and punctuation. She did not use capitals, periods, and commas conventionally. Overall, however, her spelling was quite normative, and, except for *paiz* (*país*), *heso* (*eso*), *a* (*ha*), her only other misspellings involved the use of the written accent.

In terms of content, Elisa did provide some of the information expected in a piece of writing on the topic in question. She wrote about herself and provided details about her physical appearance, her interests, and her future plans. Relationships between ideas and information, however, were not well established. Connections and transitions were lacking, and some information was incomplete or undeveloped. Overall, however, especially given the fact that writing or *redacción* was not taught in Elisa's school, she did quite well. Interestingly, in terms of content, Elisa's text reflects a view about good writing that is common among Latin Americans. This view holds that good writing should attempt to address philosophical and moral issues. In Elisa's composition, her embedded discussion about *respeto* (respect) is a manifestation of this tendency.

Beginning English-Language Abilities

Like Lilian, Elisa knew very little English when we first assessed her proficiency. She could say more words in English than could Lilian, and she could respond to questions such as *What is your name? What is your mother's name?* She could not, however, formulate those same questions herself. Elisa commented that English was very important to her mother, who insisted that both her children watch only English-language television when they were at home. Often Magda would speak to the children in English herself, telling them to close the door, go to bed, wash the dishes, and so on. Elisa was eager to learn English words in order to please her mother.

Like Lilian, Elisa could understand a lot more English than she could produce.

Interviewer: Where do you live, Elisa?
   Where do you live? Where is your house?
Elisa: Oh. My house is um. ¿Le puedo decir en español? Que cómo, me preguntó que ¿por dónde queda mi casa?   *(Understands/asks permission to respond in Spanish/ translates question)*
Interviewer: What street?
Elisa: Calderon and Case.   *(Responds)*

She was, however, a bit more advanced than Lilian and could give her telephone number in English. She could understand questions about her place of birth, nationality, and the like. Elisa was also quite able to give information about her family, including her mother, her sister, and her father (who was still in Honduras). In some cases, however, comprehension depended on my use of "foreigner talk." I deliberately simplified my language and provided hints when Elisa appeared to be confused.

Elisa found questions about her daily routine a bit more challenging:

Interviewer: What time do you get up?
  What time do you get up in the
  morning?
Elisa: A que hora me levanto por la ma-   *(Understands/translates to*
  ñana? um   *display understanding)*
Interviewer: Very good, Elisa, you under-
  stand a lot of English.
Elisa: A las seis. At six o'clock.   *(Responds to original*
                                                question)

Interviewer: And what do you do? You get
  up at six and then what?
Elisa: Um a vestirme.   *(Understands/responds in*
                                                Spanish)

Interviewer: You get dressed.   *(Interviewer translates)*
Elisa: Hacer el desayuno.   *(Continues Spanish*
                                                response)

Interviewer: Oh, you make breakfast.   *(Interviewer translates)*
Elisa: Y apago todas las luces.   *(Continues Spanish*
                                                response)

In the above exchange, Elisa seemed quite willing to engage in a bilingual conversation. She acknowledged my translations of her remarks but did not attempt to repeat them. At the end of the interview about her daily routine, Elisa admitted that there was a lot that she had not understood.

In terms of reading and writing abilities in English, Elisa's reading abilities were noticeably stronger than Lilian's. She chose an article about a young Mexican circus performer that had many illustrations of the circus, the high wire, and the net. She was able to use her real-world knowledge and cognates to obtain a general sense of the article.

By comparison, the "text" that Elisa produced in response to our request that she write in English was quite elementary.

    Elisa
    Thes tha paper   My mother is Magda
     "   "   father
     "   "   mother   family
     "   "   boy
     "   "   girl

```
"      "     baby
            door
            window
            mesuring spoon
            spatula o turner
            postre
            measurins cup
            teacher
            sister
            brother
            granmother
            name
            period
```

Elisa appeared to be unable to transfer her knowledge of writing in Spanish to writing in English. She produced a mere listing of words, both related and unrelated. She did not have either the vocabulary or the syntax that would have allowed her to do anything else.

As was the case with Lilian, at the time that the study began Elisa had very limited English-language abilities both in the oral and written modes. However, Elisa could write a connected text in her first language and could read and draw meaning from Spanish texts. Like Lilian, Elisa was willing to take chances when instructed to do so and to use existing literacy skills and her real-life knowledge to attempt to read in English.

ACCESS TO ENGLISH AT SCHOOL

As was the case with Lilian, Elisa had little or no access to her English-speaking peers at school. She was enrolled in three periods of NEP core, three sheltered courses, and a PE class during the last period of the day, as shown in Table 5.1. As compared to Lilian, however, during PE Elisa attempted to interact with students who were loners like herself, most of whom were either Asian or Asian Indian. While not in the least bit athletic, Elisa tried her best to run and to catch the ball enthusiastically and to place herself in situations in which she would be spoken to in English.

Within the NEP core itself, Elisa's access to English was as limited as Lilian's. In comparison to Lilian, however, Elisa made an effort to follow everything that was said in the classroom. She listened closely to early morning announcements over the public address system, to conversations between Mrs. Gordon and Mrs. Ayub, and—from time to time—to conversations between Mrs. Gordon and me. When I questioned her about

Table 5.1. Elisa's Schedule

Period	Classes
1	NEP core
2	NEP core
3	NEP core
4	NEP sheltered math
5	NEP sheltered science
6	NEP sheltered home arts
7	PE

how much she understood, I found that for the most part, Elisa was able to figure out the general topic of face-to-face conversations. She was less successful in identifying the topic of most school announcements.

SHELTERED CLASSES

As was the case for Lilian, Elisa's sheltered classes offered her very restricted access both to English and to the curriculum.

Math Class

The sheltered math class, taught by Justine Jackson, was perhaps Elisa's worst experience. It enrolled students who had completed algebra in Mexico; students who had completed courses equivalent to pre-algebra here; students who were less advanced but had a fairly good grasp of fractions, decimals, and the like; and students who had not yet learned the times tables.

Mrs. Jackson herself was a very cheerful and kind teacher whose gentle voice and patient manner usually disarmed even the most unruly students. She was respected by her colleagues and was thought of as a natural leader. After teaching in special education in a larger district where she had won several awards for outstanding teaching, Mrs. Jackson had moved to Garden Middle School to be near her adult daughter and her grandchildren. She was deeply invested in the sheltered math class and sought every opportunity to learn more about English-language learners.

Unfortunately, teaching subject-matter content in English to students who could neither speak nor understand the language was a very difficult task. Laudable as it was for Garden Middle School to have taken on sheltered instruction in a variety of subjects, grouping ELL students by English language ability in sheltered math presented especially serious challenges. It was not clear to me whether Justine Jackson actually had a sense of the range of the abilities she had in her class. After taking a class in sheltered techniques in which the use of simplified language and illustrations was emphasized for English-learning students, Mrs. Jackson concluded that these techniques were very similar to those used in special education. She thus volunteered to teach the sheltered math class the following year.

Mrs. Jackson approached her sheltered math class and the students from the perspective of a teacher who liked her students a great deal and who hoped to give them access to mathematics in spite of what she perceived to be their limitations. Unfortunately, Mrs. Jackson's sense of the students' limitations was not accurate. The newly arrived immigrant students were not "special" in the sense that the field of special education uses that term. They were not learning-disabled or learning-delayed; they were simply a group of 15 boys and 8 girls who did not speak English.

As a special education teacher, Mrs. Jackson was very experienced in using manipulatives, in using illustrations, and in moving slowly through material. Unfortunately the NEP students were bored by the work in the class, and they misinterpreted Mrs. Jackson's kind and loving demeanor. Used to strict, no-nonsense teachers in Mexico who were quick to use even corporal punishment, they saw Mrs. Jackson as a nice woman who did not know how to control them. The situation was made even more complex by the fact that there were indeed some students in the class who had little background in mathematics and many unruly boys who were quite advanced. There were seemingly endless opportunities to make remarks in Spanish ridiculing those who volunteered to answer a question and those who were called to the board to solve a problem. Class comedians had a field day. Even normally well-behaved students became aggressively witty. Both right and wrong answers were fed to students called upon to respond. Gullible acceptance of wrong answers met with catcalls and laughter.

Mrs. Jackson pretended to be unaware of the Spanish undercurrent that was constantly going on. She did her best to move forward patiently, following a basic general math curriculum for very low-ability sixth graders. She promised popcorn parties, excursions, and other rewards to the students if they succeeded in being quiet. From my discussions with her, I learned that, because of the students' use of Spanish in class—a language she neither spoke nor understood—she strongly felt that the students had all the power.

What is interesting to note is that for those students who had a math background, instruction in English in areas that they knew well was comprehensible. They could understand instruction on how to multiply by three-digit numbers, for example, because they had already mastered these operations in their native language long ago. The students who had no background in math, however, were clearly terrified of appearing foolish before their peers and seldom responded to requests to participate in class.

In terms of access to English, the sheltered math class offered some access to the language. Mrs. Jackson spoke slowly when she reprimanded students and used the same kinds of expressions each time. Each of her explanations was accompanied by a problem on the board to which she pointed. As is often suggested in workshops for teachers on sheltered techniques, she repeated the same concept several times. It is not difficult to imagine that students could learn language chunks (e.g., we line up the numbers one right under the other) that could be useful later. Some might argue, however, that there are far more efficient ways of learning English, especially for students who already know the concepts in question and who are being held back from developing their math abilities further.

For Elisa, the content of the class seemed to involve a review of materials that she had covered in her school in Honduras. She spoke of the class as being an easy one because it did not take up too much of her time. From time to time, however, she mentioned that she wished that the teacher would assign more homework.

Home Arts Class

The home arts class—actually a cooking class—was Elisa's favorite of all her sheltered content classes. It was taught by Mrs. Cooper, a young home economics teacher who believed strongly that cooking could provide a good solution for newly arrived students. She hoped to engage them by having them produce something that they could eat or take with them. Unfortunately, few of the Latino male students who had been placed in the class wanted to be there. They felt awkward and foolish and were clearly afraid of being ridiculed by the girls.

Elisa loved the class. The first English writing activity that she carried out for us included a list of cooking utensils. Elisa liked Mrs. Cooper and she, in turn, really liked both of the Lara sisters. A few months after school began, Elisa spoke of going to visit Mrs. Cooper at her home. Apparently, Magda and Mrs. Cooper had developed a good relationship, and Mrs. Cooper took on the role of adviser to the family. There were frequent dinners, frequent outings, and very solid advice to Magda about what to do to help her children succeed. All communication between Mrs. Cooper and Elisa was in English.

ACCESS TO THE ENGLISH-SPEAKING WORLD

Elisa's best connection to the English-speaking world was Magda. Magda was outgoing and saw herself as a fluent and effective English speaker. Through her employers and their friends, she sought to make connections for her daughters and quickly drilled them on what to say when she took them to meet different people.

Another of Elisa's strong connections to the English-speaking world was Roberto, the man whom Magda married the following year. Roberto, who was originally from Guatemala, had attended a community college and was then working on a B.S. degree in computer science. He worked as a programmer and was a fluent English speaker. He believed in education and pushed Magda herself to return to school. Roberto made it a point to talk to both Elisa and to Elvia in English. He quizzed them about what they could say, corrected their pronunciation, and made them repeat particular expressions until they could say them easily. In addition to Magda and Roberto, Elisa had access to English in a church youth organization to which she and Elvia belonged. At church activities, both girls interacted with second- and third-generation Latinas as well as with European American, English-speaking youngsters.

Compared to Lilian, Elisa had much more access to English outside of school. In spite of the fact that most of her classmates were limited-English-speaking and that the friends with whom she and her sister walked to school were also Latina and newly arrived, Elisa had many opportunities to hear English and, more importantly, to engage in genuine communication with English speakers.

ENGLISH AT THE END OF THE FIRST YEAR

As with Lilian, at the end of the first year I once again assessed Elisa's English-language ability. Compared to Lilian, Elisa had made impressive progress during the 9-month schoolyear. Her growing abilities in listening and speaking could be seen, for example, in her replies to the personal information questions.

Interviewer: Where were you born?
Elisa: Where I born? In Honduras.   *(Responds appropriately)*
Interviewer: Good, and what is your nationality?
Elisa: My nationality is from Honduras.   *(Responds appropriately)*

Interviewer: What is your favorite activity?
Elisa: In the school?   *(Asks for clarification)*
Interviewer: Anywhere.
Elisa: In the school, go to the seventh pe-   *(Responds appropriately)*
  riod. In my house. Go to my house and
  do my homework and cook.
Interviewer: Where does your mother
  work?
Elisa: She work in RepisCom. She work   *(Responds appropriately)*
  with computers. And she clean a house
  and she take care for a old man.

This same ability to participate in face-to-face interaction without major breakdowns in communication was also evident in the role-playing activities. Elisa was able to pretend to talk to a nurse at an emergency room. Although she did not have control of all the necessary vocabulary, she was able to circumlocute and otherwise continue to participate in the interaction.

Elisa's ability to produce connected discourse in English, however, was far more evident in her response to an academic listening comprehension assessment. For this part of the assessment, Elisa listened to a presentation about Hawaii in which she was asked to recall three things she had heard.

Interviewer: OK, so tell me about three
  things that you remember that I told you.
Elisa: In Hawaii some mountains have vol-   *(Recalls details)*
  canoes. And, the large, one of the name
  of the island is Honolulu?
Interviewer: . . . OK. What else?
Elisa: uhm, En Hawaii some people work   *(Recalls details)*
  producing sugar. And Hawaii is con-
  nected with the United States. And every
  year some many people go to Hawaii?
Interviewer: Good. OK, anything else you
  remember?
Elisa: They go in airplanes and boats and   *(Recalls details)*
  in boats and (mumbles something).

In terms of the written language tasks, Elisa also showed marked improvement. She was able to read a two-page text about Barbra Streisand and to produce the following text without referring to the reading.

> Barbara was a very ugly girl and she wanted
> to be a actress but her wanted to she need to be
> a secretary. Barbara wanted to learn dance but
> her don't like to her ~~dat~~ don't like to her daughter dace
> because she think the is going to break.

In this passage. Elisa attempted to reflect several key points contained in the reading: that Barbra wanted to be an actress, that her mother wanted her to be a secretary, and that her mother was afraid that if she danced, her bones would break. By itself, the text produced by Elisa is very primitive, but it is evident that Elisa understood the reading.

On the task that required Elisa to write about her school or her family, Elisa showed herself to be far more competent than she appeared to be in the summary of the reading passage.

> I like to came to the school because a
> learn a lot of English.
> and I learn to do art home a run
> the mile and a do (esperimin) and I learn. Math.
> and I learn a lot of things. and I want then
> when I be big I have a good job.
> another thing they a like to come to the school is
> because I have a lot of ~~friends~~ friends.
> And because the teaches are very good.

This particular text reflects Elisa's spoken language and her confusion between spoken and written English. The use of *a* for *I*, for example, in

> a learn a lot of English
> a do (esperimin)

revealed that she produced a schwa-like sound for the pronoun *I* in speaking. She then transcribed this sound both as *a* and *I*. Transfer of native-language syntax is also evident here. Elisa attempted to translate the Spanish subjunctive *cuando sea grande* with the English:

> and I want then when *I be* big

The text is also characterized by small errors that would have passed undetected were one listening to Elisa's rapid speech in English. For example, Elisa wrote:

another thing *they* a like to do
the *teaches* are very good

In rapid speech, these small irregularities in Elisa's English would have been insignificant. An interlocutor speaking to Elisa would probably have "heard":

another thing *that* I like to do
the *teachers* are very good

Compared to her performance 9 months before, Elisa had made outstanding progress in both oral and written language development. She saw herself as an English speaker who had some limitations but who was learning more every day. I was very pleased with her progress and fully expected that in the next academic year Elisa would be placed at a much higher level in the ESL sequence at Garden Middle School.

THE SECOND YEAR AT GARDEN MIDDLE SCHOOL

For Elisa, the second year at Garden Middle School began very much the way it had the year before. The teachers looked rested, and the students looked happy to be back at school. More new immigrant students had arrived during the summer, and the school once again faced the same crisis of trying to find classes for them. Both Mrs. Gordon and Mrs. Clayton had returned and were teaching the same NEP, LEP, and advanced LEP classes. Mrs. Emerson (the science teacher) was no longer a part of the sheltered science team. Only Mrs. Morton (science), Mrs. Jackson (math), and Mrs. Cooper (home arts) had agreed to work with entering non-English-speaking students. Other mainstream teachers had been pushed and prodded and persuaded to include immigrant students who had been at Garden for at least 1 year in their classes.

Much to my surprise, given Elisa's continued growth in English during the first year and the summer, she was once again placed in the 3-hour NEP core with Mrs. Gordon. I was especially baffled by the fact that no effort had been made to move her to Mrs. Clayton's NEP core, where she at least would not have repeated the same curriculum. Mrs. Gordon commented that although Elisa had changed over the summer and had become more of a young teen, she was not quite ready to move to a higher-level class. She informed me that since many Latino students entering from the feeder elementary schools were scoring as FES (fluent English-speaking) on the Idea Proficiency Test (IPT), she and Mrs. Clayton had decided to administer the Gates-MacGinitie Reading Test to all entering and returning students. Both she and Mrs. Clayton as well as the teacher who taught the sheltered English core class (the bridge course to mainstream English) were concerned that the IPT primarily measured interactional skills and did not offer information about the students' academic language abilities. In their opinion, the Gates-MacGinitie—because it was a test of reading—more accurately reflected students' ability to work with English-language texts and with academic language. The teachers agreed that the Gates-MacGinitie scores shown in Table 5.2 would be used for placement.

Elisa scored a total of 71 points and a grade equivalent score of 2.4, making her eligible for LEP core placement. Mrs. Gordon commented, however, that Elisa had important weaknesses in her English and would profit greatly from remaining in the NEP core for a period of time. She felt strongly that allowing students to move forward with weak skills would result in many complaints from the mainstream teachers who had agreed to take on more non-English-background students.

When I shared with her my own evaluation of Elisa's abilities and offered to let her listen to our tape-recordings of her performance, Mrs. Gordon politely thanked me but refused to further consider Elisa's placement. She did suggest, however, that she might consider moving Elisa later on during the academic year, depending on her progress.

For the first few months, then, Elisa had the schedule shown in Table 5.3. It is important to note that her enrollment in the NEP core was reduced to two periods instead of three. These two periods covered both English and social studies. Additionally, because of the intense overcrowding of the sheltered content classes, Elisa was placed in a non-ESL mainstream math course.

Hang-the-Spider—One More Time

Elisa was quite annoyed at being placed in the NEP core. She had indeed changed over the summer; the meek and shy, blend-into-the-woodwork

Table 5.2. Gates-MacGinitie Scores Used for ESL Placement

Grade Equivalent Score	Placement
1 to 1.9	NEP core
2 to 2.8	LEP core
2.9 to 3.6	Advanced LEP
3.7 and above	Sheltered English core

Table 5.3. Elisa's Schedule—The Second Year

Period	Classes
1	PE
2	NEP core
3	NEP core
4	NEP science
5	Vocal chorus (mainstream)
6	NEP home arts
7	Math (mainstream)

little girl had become a confident and much more outgoing young lady. In class, she constantly raised her hand, volunteered answers to hang-the-spider, was eager to correct punctuation errors in the daily activity involving such correction, and called out answers to general questions asked of the whole class by the teacher.

As had been the case the year before, Elisa was eager to do more work than was assigned. However, she was much less docile. When Mrs. Gordon assigned controlled compositions to the whole class, Elisa was no longer content to copy the sentences from the board exactly the way the teacher directed in order to avoid mistakes. For the first composition that the teacher assigned, for example, students produced six-sentence, almost identical texts on Koko the gorilla. Elisa, however, decided to take liberties with the text and to write her own responses to the story of Koko. Mrs. Gordon was not pleased. She skimmed Elisa's composition and pointed out to me that it had a number of very serious errors.

Over the next 2 months, Elisa continued to speak out in class, to go much beyond the teacher's assignments, and to make every effort to speak as much English as she could in Mrs. Gordon's class. What Elisa could not do was to make the class offer her more than it did. She needed the opportunity to develop her reading abilities by reading a wide variety of texts of the type she would need to read in mainstream subject-matter courses, and she needed to continue to develop her oral and written academic language. What she got instead was a repetition of many of the tasks and activities she had covered the year before.

Mrs. Gordon, on the other hand, very much enjoyed Elisa's presence and that of students like her who had been held back in her class. They became the unofficial translators, helpers, and socializers of the newly arrived immigrant students. Observing Elisa the second year, it became clear why it was important for every NEP class to be made up of at least half the students who had had the class the previous academic year. It made it possible for the teacher to speak only English to the entire class. She could depend on the more fluent members of the class to discreetly communicate necessary information to their peers.

Access to the Curriculum

As had been the case the year before, Elisa was enrolled in two sheltered classes: sheltered science and sheltered home arts. In the science class, Elisa usually sat with her friends and worked with them on group projects. The other students looked to Elisa to provide leadership. She would plan the project, assign tasks, and ultimately write whatever report needed to be handed in. Elisa seemed to have the special talent of copying full sentences and phrases from the text and from handouts that she would later incorporate into their reports. Mrs. Morton was quite aware that Elisa did most of the work in every group that she was in. Elisa greatly enjoyed the attention that she received from her peers and from the teacher. Access to English, however, was limited. Because of the presence of many students who were much less fluent than Elisa, Mrs. Morton used simple syntax and many visual aids. Students were not assigned textbooks, nor were they expected to read about the topics covered. All assignments were "hands-on" and required measuring, counting, and the like, as well as filling in charts and worksheets.

The class in vocal chorus, although in theory a mainstream class, was not a particularly rich English-language learning environment for Elisa. There was little interaction in the class, and except for the memorization of words to the songs, there was little opportunity for Elisa to expand her English-language range. The teacher appeared not to know who Elisa was and confused her with one or two of the other Latina students in the class. Elisa, however, enjoyed the class a great deal and looked forward with great excitement to the Christmas concert.

Elisa's biggest challenge was the mainstream math class. In this class, Elisa faced two main problems: (1) Mrs. Jackson's class had not given her the necessary background to do well in an eighth-grade pre-algebra class, and (2) the language demands of the class, which followed the new math standards, were quite high. From working on multiplication by four digits, Elisa moved to a class in which she was expected to plot numbers on a graph, to offer reasons for her answers, and to write carefully thought-out answers to the problems of the week. Elisa tried her best. When called on in class, she would try to respond but would often seem embarrassed when she gave the wrong answer. She would frequently call me at home in the evening for help with her homework. Often her difficulties involved the directions for completing the assignment rather than the math itself. On one occasion, for example, the assignment involved adding and subtracting fractions. However, as a self-correcting device, students were to fill in their answers in such a way that they would form a star. The directions were complicated and confusing. A second worksheet was even worse. It involved figuring out answers, entering answers at the bottom of a worksheet, crossing out some of the answers in a particular pattern, and using the letters not crossed out to figure out a secret code. Elisa was frustrated and upset, and her mother was quite fearful that she would become dependent on getting outside help. I was soon told not to help Elisa when she called.

Several months into the schoolyear, Elisa was transferred to another mainstream math class. The change was due to the fact that she had been moved from the NEP to the LEP core. Nevertheless, the change was disorienting. Elisa had to adjust to a new teacher and new classmates. She continued to struggle with the mathematics itself as well as with directions for word problems. Figures 5.1 and 5.2 are examples of the kinds of answers that Elisa handed in to the required problem of the week.

In the text shown in Figure 5.2, Elisa selected a practical, familiar situation (shopping at Target) to explain the relationship in question. Her writing had a number of problems, and it was non-native-like in many respects. More importantly, perhaps, as compared to the writings handed in by her peers, Elisa's was quite brief. It did not reflect the many hours that she had spent carefully composing her answer.

Not surprisingly, Elisa did not get a good grade in the class. She received a C+ because Mrs. Heinz did not believe that Elisa understood basic

---

Figure 5.1. Elisa's Response to Problem of the Week

Math 2°   Elisa Lara
                                                      2/10/93

Explain, show, or demonstrate the relationship between ½ and 50%. Do this in as many different ways as you can.

She draws 4 of these proportions

The relationship between ½ and 50% is that 50% of 1 pizza is the same than ½ of one pizza. 50% is half something, ½ is half of something too.

Figure 5.2. Elisa's Response to Percent Problem

"Problem"

I only have forty dollars and I want to buy a pair of jeans and a T shirt. If I go to Target and I see a pair of jeans that cost forty dollars, but now is on sale for 50% off. That means that the jeans cost half of the forty dollars, because 50% means half of something. I saw a T shirt over there in the corner that cost fourty dollars, but now is 1/2 off. That means the same thing as 50% did for the jeans. Now I got what I wanted, I have a pair of jeans, a T shirt, and I only spent forty dollars. cool!!

---

concepts. Elisa was disappointed and argued that she had worked very hard. She had spent hours on the math portfolio, copying whole sections from books on geometrical figures. At the end, it was not as complete as the teacher had wanted, and she was graded down for copying and including what appeared to be memorized material. Mrs. Heinz recommended that the following year Elisa be enrolled in LEP algebra as opposed to mainstream algebra.

English at the End of the Second Year

In spite of Elisa's struggle in the math class, the experience was very important in developing her reading and writing abilities in English. More importantly, perhaps, it allowed her to interact with English-speaking peers for the first time. At the end of the second year, I once again assessed Elisa's English-language ability using the same procedures used in the three previous assessments as well as a variety of other tasks. She confidently answered all personal questions and added personal comments and elaborations. She was successful in role-playing the part of a customer at a store, a customer at a restaurant, and a patient in a hospital emergency room. She read all materials presented to her with ease and provided summaries of content contained therein. She produced the following writing sample for this assessment, included below.

MY IDEAL DAY
I woke up on Saturday morning, it was cold
and dark. I had breakfast with my sister,
mom and dad. I knew that that day I
was going to have fun. My mom and dad

were getting ready to go to work and my
sister to go out with her friends.
When everybody had already left it was
about six-thirty a.m. I started getting ready.
I went in the shower and spent 30 minutes.
When I got out of the shower it was
about 7:00 AM. I put lotion all over my
body and put on my favorite underwear,
pair of jeans, T.shirt, jacket and pair of
shoes, I was feeling fresh and clean,
I guess I was ready.
I phoned my friend Rolando to tell
him that I was ready. I wait for him
for ten minutes. When I saw him coming,
I saw a big limosine too. He asked me;
"do you want to come in"? I said yes.
We went to San Francisco, we stay
there for almost two hour. There we
ate another funer breakfast.
I asked him if he wanted to go
shopping with me. He answer yes. We
went to almost all the malls in San
Francisco. We spent almost all morning
and part of the afternoon shopping.
Then we went for a big dinner at Sizzler.

Elisa's writing changed dramatically between the end of the first year
and the second year. However, it is important to point out that the text
Elisa produced during this assessment was not an entirely spontaneous
piece of writing. She had been working on several versions of a similar
piece of writing for quite some time.

By the end of the second year, we had also collected a number of other
texts written by Elisa for other classes. The following two examples illustrate the development of her written English-language abilities. Elisa wrote
the first text and turned it in to her science teacher for extra credit.
She wrote the second text to a special friend in her church group with
whom she communicated mainly in writing. Text appears exactly as Elisa
wrote it.

Text 1
Silicon Ghaprics it a big company this company has a lot of
buildings, we went to two buildings first we went to building sis,

and the people who works there, they take us to a room where
the presidents of the company has they meatings. And then we
divide us in two groups and then my group went to the second
building that was building two. They call building two Human

Factors

Lab

in building two they talk what the company made? The campany
made computers, and they also talk about what they do in
building two. What they do is to test people to see how they do
in computers. And they ask if someone of us wanted to try to do
the test. Then we went to a room and there was two big t.v.'s and
we was watching at him doing the test. And then we went to
building to again and then I have the chance to play with the
computer and it's very easy to play in that computer it was a very
nice expeirence to meat people, learnd about computers They
tell us some of the activitis they do. Every year competitive of
the best video of the year. They show
us the video and there was very good.
I like did we meat some workers, there was the
person who made the aplications her name is Mimi Celis. The
secretery's name is Clara Colon. The engineer name is Pablo
Sanches. The manufacturing's name is Velia Rico. The security's
name is Hank Sisneros. All they tall us something about ther life.
Dwayne Corneleas/Product Demo.
Hi talk's about the Iris Iudigo, and then hi show us a video about
Moviemaking Tirers
T.V.   Safety
Medical   Video
There are made it with computers
Hi also talk about his life.

TEXT 2

friend is a big gift that life give to people
And here I got, one of the bigest pressents,
you has a friend

If you could see trough my heart you would see a
light shining every singale minute that I
think about you
this light means our friendship our beautiful
friend ship. And my heart and me, have
decidedo to keep it.

And you know way? ~~We have dicided to keep it?~~
~~WELL~~ becouse
you have been very nice ~~to me and very kind~~
and cool. to me
~~has never someone haven do that before~~
I hope we can be best friends for our whole life
Please don't let this light inside of me go away.

In sum, at the end of her second year in this country, Elisa could display information, recount events, express opinions, and express feelings both orally and in writing. From an ESL perspective—that is, if one compares Elisa to most Latino students who have been here for only 2 years—her performance was exceptional. Some ESL teachers, however, would possibly be concerned about her lack of grammatical accuracy. Others, seeing the continued acquisition of English structures without direct instruction, would feel confident that many of her errors would disappear over time. From a mainstream perspective, Elisa's writing was definitely non-native-like. Many regular English teachers, especially those who are not used to reading the writing of incipient and developing bilinguals, would perhaps not appreciate what Elisa had accomplished on her own or what she might be able to accomplish with appropriate instruction.[1]

PLANNING FOR HIGH SCHOOL

For eighth-graders at Garden School, planning for the next year began in February and March. Because of the very large number of ESL students at Garden, administrators at the two area high schools had agreed that in odd-numbered years all entering ESL students would be sent to Mission Vista High School; in even-numbered years, all entering students would be sent to Los Verdes High School. In this way, both high schools would enroll approximately the same number of ESL students.

In 1993, arrangements were made for the eighth-grade class to attend Mission Vista High. Recommendations for placement for mainstream students were made by each respective teacher for math, science, and English. ESL students were recommended for placement by their ESL teachers. ESL teacher recommendations overruled those of subject-matter teachers.

Elisa was excited about enrolling at Mission Vista and quite certain that she would mainstreamed for all her classes. She knew that she had made a great deal of progress in English and looked forward to starting high school and doing well. She had already begun to think about college and asked many questions about what courses had to be taken and in what order. Unfortunately, Mrs. Gordon recommended that Elisa be placed, once again, in the ESL track at the high school level. She did not support Elisa's placement in mainstream classes—not because of the level of her proficiency in English, but because Elisa had not completed the last book in the ESL textbook series used at Garden.

Needless to say, both Elisa and her mother were discouraged. At Mission Vista, the ESL track included many levels of ESL and a number of designated ESL subject-matter (sheltered) courses. At that time, no ESL classes or sheltered classes met college entrance requirements.

6

Manolo

Manolo was a tall, good-looking youngster who towered over most of his classmates. He had a pleasant baby-face and a serious and respectful demeanor that made most teachers like him. He was both a large child, who enjoyed riding his bicycle with his cousin and playing with tiny cars, as well as an adolescent, who was quite aware of the girls around him. In Mexico, Manolo had completed sixth grade. He could describe his classes in some detail and was happy to talk about his plans for the future. In love with planes, he wanted to become an Air Force pilot and to fly very large planes. He seemed confident and articulate.

When the study began, Manolo was only 12 years old and already about 5 feet 10 inches tall. He had arrived in Mission Vista from Mexico City during the summer. Manolo, his mother Rita, and his 16-year-old sister Estela had moved to California to be with his father, who had been working here for 2 years. Manolo's 18-year-old brother Anselmo had followed his father to California a year previously.

In Mexico, Omar Fuentes had been a *policía de tránsito* (a member of the transit police force) who had his own police car. Additionally, he had had a business selling electrical appliances on the side. After 17 years on the force, and after having lived a largely middle-class existence in the country's capital, Omar had serious problems with his superior. As a result, he lost his car and was demoted. Angry and outraged at the way he had been treated, he left the police force and came to the United States. Rita lamented the fact that her husband had needed only 5 more years to qualify for a lifetime pension. "No se quiso quedar" (He didn't want to stay), she said sadly. "Es demasiado orgulloso" (He is much too proud).

When Omar arrived in Mission Vista, his two brothers—who were already in the area—took bets on how long he would stay. They saw Omar as soft, used to having money, and incapable of working as hard as new immigrants work in California. Rita smiled as she bragged that Omar had proved them all wrong. He had worked two and three jobs, his employers liked him, and he would soon be able to buy a small mobile home for his family. Omar was determined that here, too, they would live in a house that belonged to them.

The family lived in a large apartment complex on the main street of the immigrant sector in Mission Vista. There was a clear difference between this complex and those in which both the Duque and the Lara families lived. The yards were neatly kept, the swimming pool was surrounded by padded garden chairs, and areas surrounding the pool area and leading to the apartments were carpeted with artificial turf.

Rita Fuentes was a young-looking, heavy-set woman who wore her hair pulled back in a bun at the back of her neck. She wasn't sure that she wanted to stay in Mission Vista, in California, or in the United States. She admitted that she was very lonely and that she spent most of her time by herself. She talked a great deal about the weight-loss support group to which she had belonged in Mexico City and about learning how to be responsible for herself. She also spoke about belonging to a Christian group called *Sígueme* (Follow Me). Rita was eager to learn English and attended adult school for classes from 9:00 A.M. to noon and from 6:00 to 9:00 P.M. every day. She mentioned that she avoided the students in the class who spoke Spanish and sat with the Asian students.

Overall, Rita had little to say about Manolo, except that he was 12 and that she was not pleased with the school that he had attended in Mexico City. Apparently the area where they had lived had had bad schools, with teachers who really did not care. She claimed that Manolo had learned everything he knew by third grade.

Rita was much more worried about her daughter Estela. In order to convince her to come to California, Rita had brought her boyfriend as well. Now they were both in school and in trouble because they were frequently absent. Rita was quite distressed but understood that her daughter did not like school. She confided that she had not told her husband that the principal wanted to meet with them because she feared that he would seek the advice of his brothers and their wives—all of whom spoke good English. Rita did not want to appear ignorant and uninformed in their eyes or to admit that bringing the boyfriend had not been a good idea.

Compared to Lilian's and Elisa's families, Manolo and his family enjoyed many advantages. Rita could stay at home and enroll for English classes because her son and her husband were both working. Moreover, because the family had relatives in the area, they had access to a great deal of information about how things worked in this country.

IN THE CLASSROOM

Manolo was very well liked by Mrs. Gordon, Mrs. Ayub, and his other teachers. He was well behaved and kept mainly to himself. During whole-class activities, he eagerly raised his hand and called out answers. He was self-assured and saw himself as knowing just a bit more than his peers. Often, he would look around to see if anyone else had raised his or her hand to respond to a question, and upon determining that no one had, he would quickly respond. He smiled broadly when Mrs. Gordon praised him. Reluctant to help other students during group work, he read other materials and did not engage in interactions with his less proficient classmates. In part because he did not do group work at the right time, he was often late in handing in assignments. Mrs. Gordon's appraisal of Manolo was that he was bright but lazy. My appraisal was that he was bright but bored.

Reading and Writing in Spanish

When we assessed his ability to read in Spanish, Manolo chose a second-grade textbook. I was somewhat surprised that he chose such an easy book, but he read a segment out loud confidently and then summarized what he had read briefly but competently. Surprisingly, given his general self-confidence, Manolo's writing seemed very elementary. This text is laid out as Manolo wrote it.

> Manolo Fuentes bino a los Estados Unidos en 199_
> En pese a benir a la escuela alprinsipio me
> sentia mal porque cuando salia a la calle
> ablavan muchas personas en ingles y llono
> en ten dia lo que desian le echeganas al
> ingles y aora en tiendo se pedircosa en
> ingles y mesiento vien pienso esforsarme
> en el ingles y la escuela y rregresar a
> Mexico cuando sea grande por a ora seguir
> en la escuela y estudiar mucho

> [Manolo Fuentes came to the United States in 199_.
> I began to come to school at first
> I felt bad because when I went out in the street
> many people spoke English and I didn't
> understand what they said I put effort into
> English and now I understand I know how to ask for

things in English and I feel good I plan to work hard
at English and at school and to return to
Mexico when I'm older for now stay
in school and study a lot]

In terms of form, the text produced by Manolo was much less competent in some respects than that produced by Elisa. Manolo did not punctu-
ate sentences, nor did he use sentence-initial capital letters. He made no
attempt to use the written accent. He also produced a very large number
of incorrectly segmented words, for example *llono* (for *yo no*), *en pese* (for
empecé), *en ten dia* (for *entendía*), *echeganas* (for *eché ganas*), *en tiendo*
(for *entiendo*), *mesiento* (for *me siento*), and *a ora* (for *ahora*). Word-seg-
mentation errors such as these are generally typical of first- and second-
graders, not of students of *primero de secundaria* (seventh grade) like Manolo. Other errors, however, involving confusion between *b* and *v* *(benir,
bine, ablavan, vien)*, confusion between *s*, *c*, and *z* *(em pese, prinsipio,
desian, esforsarme)*, confusion between *ll* and *y* *(llono)*, and misuse of *h* *(a
ora)*, are quite typical of many youngsters in elementary school (first
through sixth grades) and even of adults with low literacy skills. The use
of double *rr* *(rregresar)* in word-initial position is not as common.

In terms of content, Manolo did write on the assigned topic. Examined
as an informative paper following Gentile (1992), his paper can be considered to include a limited amount of information as well as an attempt to
relate several pieces of the information given. There is a sense of purpose
in the writing as well as a focus.

Beginning English-Language Abilities

In terms of his oral language abilities, Manolo was far more advanced
than the other three focal students. In our first assessment of his English
proficiency, he was quite capable of providing all information asked for
(personal, family, daily routine). We thus proceeded to the role-playing
activities (pretend you are a customer in a store, pretend you are sick and
are at the emergency room, pretend you want to make a long-distance
collect call). A segment of the first role play is included below.

Interviewer: Hello. Good morning.
Manolo: Good morning. How much is   *(Initiates request for infor-*
   here this little toy.   *mation)*
Interviewer: This little toy? That's five
   ninety-eight.

Manolo: Five ninety-eight. Or this one?   *(Keeps communication go-*
                                                  ing/initiates other request
                                                  for information)

Interviewer: This one is, I think it's twelve
  ninety-five. Let me look. Yes, twelve
  ninety-five. This is very good.
Manolo: Oh yeah.   *(Signals understanding)*
Interviewer: It's French. It's a French toy.
Manolo: OK.
Interviewer: This is a Mexican toy. *(point-*
  ing to the first toy)
Manolo: OK. I like the food. Where is the   *(Changes subject)*
  food?
Interviewer: The food. We don't have very
  much food here. We have some sodas
  and we have some potato chips, but we
  don't have food.
Manolo: OK. Where is the candy? Candy.   *(Changes request)*

As will be noted, although I fell into clear use of foreigner talk, Manolo's understanding did not appear to be dependent on such language
simplification. He was able to maintain open lines of communication in his
role as a customer in a small store.

For the reading part of the assessment, Manolo, like Elisa, chose the
article on the young circus performer. He read silently, but his summary
revealed that he had understood almost the entire article. He recalled even
small details, and he was able to comment extensively on the young performer.

In comparison to Lilian and Elisa, Manolo's English writing was much
more sophisticated. Rather than producing a list of unrelated words, Manolo attempted to talk about Halloween. The text he produced had many
misspellings (*naigt, strets, Hallowen, ay [I]*), but he was able to express
two ideas: (1) that on Halloween people go out to ask for candy and (2)
that people wear masks of many types.

> This is the naigt the Hallowen much people go to the strets for
> candies much people have mask the mommy, bat, or dracula ay like
> mask the bat or much more mask.

ACCESS TO ENGLISH AT SCHOOL

Like Lilian and Elisa, Manolo had very little access to English at school.
He, too, was enrolled in the NEP core for three periods. His other courses

were sheltered ones—sheltered math with Mrs. Jackson, sheltered computers, and sheltered science. In his PE course Manolo made no effort to interact with English-speaking students.

The entire time that he was at school, Manolo moved from class to class with the other ELL students. He spent both his morning break and his lunchtime recess with students who lived near him and with whom he rode to school every morning on his bicycle. All these boys were newly arrived as well.

SHELTERED CLASSES

Manolo's sheltered classes gave him very little access to English and very little access to content. His science class, for example, was a special disappointment to him. He actually had an extraordinary teacher, but the challenges she faced in making subject matter understandable to less motivated and less interested ELL students made it impossible for her to devote special attention to Manolo.

The teacher, Yuka Morton, who had arrived in this country as a monolingual Japanese-speaking teenager, planned every bit of her lessons by enlisting the help of Spanish-speaking friends and colleagues. She patiently explained very difficult concepts by drawing on overhead slides in several colors and actually engaged students in carrying out experiments. At the beginning of the year, however, she found it very difficult to keep the students' attention. In spite of her efforts, students' English-language ability was simply not at the level where they could actually learn concepts or understand explanations.

Throughout the year, observations of Manolo in Mrs. Morton's NEP science class revealed that the teacher made extraordinary efforts to engage students' attention and to use comprehensible English. On good days, some of the more serious students, including Manolo, made an effort to understand and to stay on-task. Most of the time, however, the teacher struggled to maintain control of the class. Very few of the students understood any English at all. They listened for a short time; they made an attempt to understand; and they soon became exhausted by the effort involved in trying to listen to extensive segments of English. They were easily distracted. When the teacher attempted to explain a concept using overheads and pictures, and as she asked for student feedback, an especially unruly group of youngsters made comments aloud in Spanish. These remarks were intended to be funny, and, in general, they had the desired effect. Students would break into laughter and would respond, returning insults and humorous remarks. Mrs. Morton tried her best to maintain order by varying class activities, by providing stimulating opportunities for hands-on science, and the like, but during most of the year, the unruly students created disruptions almost daily. Manolo angrily stared down at his desk when explanations were interrupted. Several times he was particularly disappointed and commented that he really wanted to know the results of the experiment that the teacher had begun.

ACCESS TO THE ENGLISH-SPEAKING WORLD

Outside of school, Manolo had access to the English-speaking world through his father's family, who had been in the country for many years. Both of his father's brothers spoke English well, and one had a wife who, while of Mexican background, spoke only English. All their children spoke English almost exclusively. When Manolo spent time with his cousins on weekends, the language of interaction was normally English. Manolo's mother commented that although Manolo might not understand everything that was being said, he would act as though he had understood.

Manolo spoke fondly of a cousin with whom he would go on long bicycle rides exploring Mission Vista. He also spoke admiringly of his brother, Anselmo, who was—after a single year in the United States—able to use English at his job.

ENGLISH AT THE END OF THE FIRST YEAR

By May of the first year, Manolo was quite capable of communicating a number of different meanings in English both orally and in writing. During the second language assessment, for example, he wrote two texts. One text responded to a reading about Michael Jackson, and the other text talked about his early experiences in the United States. In the first text, Manolo expressed his opinion about Michael Jackson and supported this opinion by giving reasons for liking him. He communicated his thoughts quite clearly.

> I like Michael Jackson because I like
> ohw he dance he's very good dancing
> some times I want to dance like him
> And he's good singing too

The same growing communicative ability was evident in the other text that Manolo wrote.

> When I came to the US in the airplane I was
> skare because I think it's going to be fun.

> But when you're here it's hard you don't no
> about. The first day when I come to school
> was fun because I can't find the rooms
> it was fun. When I'm in my home it's
> different I do my homework and I go out
> with my bysicle I go out I go very far
> away from by home and I think like a eagle
> I want to fly because I really want to
> fly. In the future I want to worck in the airforce.

In this text, Manolo displayed his rapidly developing oral proficiency in English by using a set of learned expressions that he produced in his spoken language. Like Elisa, Manolo's increasing fluency in writing was related to his increasing oral language competency.

There are a number of peculiar elements in this text. The overuse of the phrases *it's going to be fun* and *it was fun* suggest either that Manolo did not truly understand the meaning of these phrases or that he was using them as filler when he could not think of anything else to say. In spoken interaction, the use of such phrases, especially among young people, often suggests fluency and familiarity with English that may not truly be present.

By the end of the first year, then, Manolo had developed the ability to write what he could already say. He could participate in conversations about himself; answer personal questions; and role-play the part of a customer, a patient in an emergency room, and an individual making a collect call. He could also summarize what he had read in English, producing both a brief English summary and a more detailed summary in Spanish.

THE SECOND YEAR AT GARDEN SCHOOL

As was pointed out in the discussion of Elisa's placement during the second year at Garden School, in the fall of the second year, placement testing was carried out using both the IPT and the Gates-MacGinitie Reading Test. Manolo obtained a total of 81 points and a grade equivalent score of 3.6. This score made him eligible for advanced LEP with Mrs. Clayton and gave him the schedule shown in Table 6.1.

Manolo began the year in three regular or mainstream classes: science, social studies, and math. He also enrolled in beginning Spanish. Except for English, all of Manolo's courses were with mainstream, fluent English-speaking students and taught by teachers who were not expected to modify their instruction to accommodate the English-language limitations of ESL students. In part because of the abrupt change from sheltered classes to

Table 6.1. Manolo's Schedule—The Second Year

Period	Classes
1	PE 7–8
2	Spanish I 7–8
3	Social studies 7
4	Science 7
5	Math (advanced) 7
6	Advanced LEP 6–8
7	Advanced LEP 6–8

mainstream classes, Manolo seemed to experience some difficulties in both social studies and science. He spent hours reading his textbooks and completing homework. Since his ESL class had provided him with no experience in extensive reading, he was forced to work on developing reading skills by himself at the same time that he was also attempting to learn subject matter. Moreover, since his NEP social studies class the previous year had not been directed at filling in his many knowledge gaps, he knew little about American history. He did not recognize the names of the founding fathers; he had never heard of the Boston Tea Party; and he did not know even the basics about American government. Strong as his developing language skills were, he felt discouraged because he was far behind his peers in many important ways.

Mainstream classes presented other difficulties as well. In Vicky Emerson's regular science class, for example, Manolo found himself in an innovative, hands-on class that required students to work in groups and to carry out a set of different exploratory activities (e.g., designing gliders on a computer, making timelines, measuring the speed at which paper airplanes fell to the ground). Student talk in each group centered around the particular task to be carried out but also involved a lot of social interaction. The group to which Manolo was assigned included two European-American young men—who were highly motivated and interested in science—and Manolo. Since Manolo was clearly very different from his peers, they treated him with thinly disguised impatience. For the most part, they simply ignored him as they quickly moved to finish the task on which the entire group would be graded. Manolo was included only when Ms. Emerson circulated and specifically asked Manolo a question or determined whether he, too, had had a turn using the computer. In the science class, Manolo, in theory, had access to English from native-speaking peers. This English, however, was not directed at him.

THE TRANSFER TO J.F.K. MIDDLE SCHOOL

By the end of October, Manolo's family had bought a mobile home and moved from Mission Vista. Manolo transferred to J.F.K. Middle School, located in a more affluent community where the ethnic-minority population (African American and Latino) was less than 2 percent.

The ESL program at J.F.K. School was designed and implemented for the children of professionals, not for newly arrived working-class immigrants of Latino background. Typically, ESL classes at J.F.K. enrolled one or two students of Latino background and many students of European, Chinese, Japanese, Korean, Scandinavian, and Israeli backgrounds. During the year of the study, the school had experienced an influx of Russian children.

J.F.K. Middle School, moreover, was very unlike Garden Middle School in its philosophy toward ESL students. At J.F.K., non-English-speaking students were considered to be bright and well educated and suffering from the temporary handicap of not knowing English. ESL classes were designed to help students develop the kinds of academic language skills that they would need to succeed in the mainstream curriculum as soon as possible. Students—who were often the children of distinguished scientists—were considered to be college-bound by school personnel in general. ESL was seen as a necessary support sequence for students who were also enrolled in mainstream courses. To help students keep up with their academic work in such courses, individual tutors were available in a number of languages (e.g., Russian, Hebrew). Tutors generally accompanied newly arrived students to class, took notes for them, and later helped them keep up with their assignments.

What was taken for granted at J.F.K. was that ELL students were eager to learn, that they had been good students in their own countries, and that they had mainstream, middle-class views about education. The isolation of ELL students that existed at Garden School did not occur at J.F.K. ELL students interacted mainly with one another, to be sure, but they interacted primarily in English. Moreover, mainstream students seemed comfortable with limited-English-speaking students and even with the accompanying tutors who took notes for newly arrived youngsters.

English-language instruction even for beginning ESL students was designed to move them rapidly in their English-language development. The beginning ESL teacher, for example, deliberately planned assignments that required students to interview their fluent English-speaking schoolmates about a variety of topics. This same class included a unit on the exploration of the Americas that required students to learn about the early American explorers as well as to sharpen their listening, note-taking, and reporting skills. As opposed to focusing exclusively on structures and vocabulary, beginning ESL at J.F.K. sought to develop students' listening, reading, writing, and speaking skills for academic purposes. Rather than a bottom-up approach to language teaching, the program reflected a belief that students could be taught to draw meaning from both oral language and texts even if they did not understand every element of the discourse in question.

MANOLO AT J.F.K.

Obtaining permission to follow Manolo at J.F.K. School was not simple. School personnel wanted to make certain that Manolo still wanted to be a part of the study. They consulted with Manolo's parents and with Manolo quite extensively. Unfortunately, these procedures led to Manolo's feeling singled out in a new context among new people. The result was that, even though Manolo finally agreed to continue in the study, he was much less cooperative than he had been at Garden Middle School. I was limited to observing his classes and to making copies of materials he produced in class that his teachers were willing to share with us. During the schoolyear, I had little personal contact with Manolo, and, in observing all of his classes, I made certain that he did not feel conspicuous or singled out. When he said that he was not willing to have his English-language development assessed by the research team during the second year, I did not press him further. I thus have no second-year language assessment data for Manolo that parallels the data collected on his language development during the first year.

In spite of these limitations, however, I was able to observe Manolo and to get a good sense of his English-language development from his performance in class. In the ESL class (called English language development [ELD]), I was able to get an excellent sense of the development of his English writing abilities by making photocopies of two journals produced during the academic year as well as other class projects and materials.

During the first semester of the second year, Manolo's schedule included the classes shown in Table 6.2. During the second semester, his schedule changed to the one shown in Table 6.3.

THE ESL CLASS AT J.F.K.

The ESL—or ELD—class into which Manolo was placed at J.F.K. was an advanced seventh- and eighth-grade class taught by Pamela Samuels. Mrs. Samuels, also a mainstream English teacher at J.F.K., was an experienced professional whose every gesture reflected a profound respect for her stu-

Table 6.2. Manolo's Schedule at J.F.K.

Period	Classes
1	Computers
2	Science
3	Math
4	Creative writing
5	PE
6	ELD
7	ELD

dents. In talking about her class, she stated that her goal in teaching advanced ELD in middle school was to mainstream students *before* they got into high school. She added that, in many cases, she worked hard to place students in her own regular mainstream English classes so that they might make the transition more easily.

The ELD class itself covered some of the elements of the core curriculum (e.g., reading *Tom Sawyer*), traditional English grammar as taught to native speakers (e.g., study of adverbial clauses, use of the present progressive, punctuation), and writing. Each class began with a segment of about 10 minutes in which students wrote in their journals in response to a teacher prompt. Mrs. Samuels generally talked for a few minutes as students prepared to write in their journals and suggested ways in which students might respond. She allowed students to work for 5 to 10 minutes and then collected journals. During the week, she responded to what stu-

Table 6.3. Manolo's Schedule—Second Semester

Period	Classes
1	Adolescent skills
2	Keyboarding
3	Math
4	PE
5	Industrial technology
6	ELD
7	ELD

dents had written. Often students used preliminary thoughts written in their journals as starting points for longer assignments.

Mrs. Samuels gave much attention to the writing of several long papers on various topics. These papers were written over a period of time and went through several drafts, including a draft prepared in response to writing conferences. During the spring, Mrs. Samuels taught students how to write a paper that would speculate about an effect. This type of paper was one of the writing tasks on which mainstream eighth-graders would be tested. Mrs. Samuels believed that it was very important for ESL students to write similar papers.

Mrs. Samuels began work on the speculative paper by explaining what the students would write about and how they would organize their paper. She selected as a title for their papers "A Decade of Difference." She then explained that the paper would have three parts by showing an overhead containing the segments shown in Figure 6.1.

Students worked on this paper for about 4 weeks. During that time, journal writing focused them on thinking about the paragraphs they would include in the speculative paper. On one occasion, for example, Mrs. Samuels prompted the students as follows:

> Remember I asked you to think about who you are right now. Where you live. Who you live with. What you like to do. What you're good at. What makes you happy. What makes you sad. Think for just a minute right now, just sit there and be aware of your body. Pencils down. Don't answer, just think. Pretend you're in that 1983 body. What it can do and what it can't do. Pencils down.

After hearing this general reminder and overview, students were asked to cluster ideas about their 1983 bodies and to share them with partners.

Many other activities were carried out during the course of writing the speculative paper. These included writing first drafts, participating in a writing conference with the teacher and other adults (including visitors to the classroom like myself), sharing drafts with fellow students, and revising and preparing the final draft, which was to be graded by the teacher. The final draft of Manolo's speculation-about-effects paper is shown in Figure 6.2.

As will be noted, in teaching ESL students to write a challenging paper, Mrs. Samuels used a combination of strategies. She gave students a general scaffold or structure for the paper as a whole and thereby taught a great deal about organization. She also prompted students to think and to write spontaneously about themselves and their lives, and she showed them how to use initial clustering techniques and note-taking to move to the writing

Figure 6.1. Organization Guidelines for Speculative Essay

A Decade of Difference

So many things can happen in 10 years. Often 10 years can bring positive changes; 10 years can also result in differences and negative situations.

In 1983, I was _____ years old and I _____
(Here's where you will use the paragraph you already wrote. Some things may need to be changed.)

Today in 1993, I am _____ years old and _____
(Here's where you'll talk about yourself today and the changes that have occurred to you. You may have had some real family changes, such as new babies, weddings, divorces.)

I can only guess what life will be like in 10 years, but I do have a dream for 2003. If my dream comes true in 2003, I will _____
(There should be some detail here. It should be about what you will do. This is where you will put in your paragraph of what you hope will happen.)

If my dream comes true, there will be both positive and negative effects.
      negative effects
      positive effects

Conclusion

of a first draft. She emphasized the steps in the writing process and used both writing conferences and peer response groups. She encouraged students to take responsibility for improving their writing in response to both peer and teacher feedback.

As compared to both Mrs. Gordon and Mrs. Sikorsky (Lilian's teacher), Mrs. Samuels did not believe that teaching ESL involved primarily teaching structures. She pushed students to use their English proficiencies, limited though they might still be, to write about real experiences and to express genuine thoughts. She adapted a process approach to writing so that students who were not totally familiar with the conventions of English writing might learn how to organize their writing in ways in which they would be expected to do so in mainstream classes.

In addition to teaching writing in her class, Mrs. Samuels also covered the novel *Tom Sawyer*. Students were expected to read segments of the work individually, but the novel was also read in class, with students taking the parts of different characters and reading their "lines" aloud. Before beginning the reading, Mrs. Samuels would recall the action in the story and would attempt to interest students in what might happen next. As students read, she frequently called attention to particular lexical items that might be confusing (e.g., *ferry* vs. *fairy*). She also provided important bits of cultural background knowledge that students probably would not know (e.g., facts about the Mississippi River, facts about riverboats and rafts).

A segment of the ELD two-period core class also included social studies. For this segment, Mrs. Samuels used a variety of approaches for developing both an understanding of the content and English-language skills. During the first semester, for example, the class focused on the study of different areas of the world. Guest speakers were invited to the class, and students were expected to take notes from these presentations and to write summaries of what they had heard. Students also read about these countries and studied some aspects of their artistic production.

During the second semester, the class focused on U.S. history, using the text *We the People*. The teacher used a number of different strategies for helping students to read the class text and to remember key facts. One strategy involved students' using a teacher-prepared checklist to focus their reading. Other approaches involved teaching students how to use chapter questions to find facts in the text, how to underline key information, how to skim and scan, and how to talk about information that they found in the text. Frequently, students were asked to read particular segments of the text and to share with the class "something that they should remember."

Mrs. Samuels also included a number of American classics in her teaching. During the second semester, for example, students read the poem "Casey at the Bat." The teacher used this as an opportunity to teach aspects of American culture, including baseball—how it works, how it is played, and the fact that it is known as the great American pastime.

In sum, Manolo's ESL class at J.F.K. School was a master class. The teacher understood both the demands of mainstream classes and what she needed to do to help students develop the English-language proficiency needed to succeed academically in such classes. Moreover, because she worked in a setting where a non-English background was not assumed to be indicative of limitations of innate talent or ability, Mrs. Samuels saw her students as intelligent, talented, and capable of learning both subject matter and language.

Figure 6.2. Manolo's Speculation-About-Effects Paper

SPECULATION	ENGLISH 6–7
ABOUT EFFECTS	MANOLO FUENTES

So many things can happen in ten years. Often, ten years can bring positive changes; Ten years can also provide difficult and negative situations.

In 1983, I was four years old. I was a little chubby. I had black hair and I was not very tall then, I like to be heald and everybody liked to hold me. I lived with my parents, one brother and one sister. I'm the youngest one. I used to move a lot in my country and go on trips with my family. What I liked to do in those days was play all day, eat, and watch T.V. I didn't care about anything else.

In 1993 I'm thirteen years old, I have changed a lot in the last ten years. Now I care about manythings. I care about school, myself, and other people. Now I just don't like to play all day, there are many other things that I like to do. I like do homework, eat, play, and watch T.V. I might make my bed or cean room and I also care about how I look.

I can only guess what my life will be like in ten years. By 2003 my dream is to became a soldier or a marine, what I want to do there is learn new things and get to see new places. By that time I would have graduated from J.F.K. and and I might have played basketball in the school team, and also I will graduated from GREEN and maybe in that time I would have played some kind of musical intrument in the band, and by that time I will also have graduated from College and there I would have played basketball and music.

If my dream comes through positive things that can happen arc that I will have been a good soldier or a good marine. I might have got to see new places and got lots of new frinends, and I would have learned lot's of new things.

If my dream coome through negative things that can happen might be that I might not get to see my family for a long time. and I might not be able to spend time for my self like going on vacations and have lot's of fun just by my self.

When I was a kid I didn't care about many things. There was some body else to take care of porblems and other things. But now, as I grow it seems that is almost my turn to do it. That's why I have to get ready for the future. that's why I get to do more new things, that's why I get more responsibilities and tha's why I have to learn lot's of new things for the future Tha's why now I have to choose what I want to be so I can start making my own life. I want to become somebody and to fell, like somebody.

THE TEACHING OF OTHER SUBJECT MATTER AT J.F.K.

Except for the ESL classes, Manolo's classes at J.F.K. were mainstream, that is, they were designed for fluent or native-English-speaking students. Manolo's science class, for example, included both explanations and hands-on group work, report writing, and multiple-choice tests. His math class reflected the new thinking in math instruction and involved students in hypothesizing, problem solving, and talking about problem solving. Computation was generally considered secondary, and students were encouraged to use calculators in class. The creative writing class was relaxed and supportive, and the young teacher encouraged students to experiment and be creative with language.

PROGRESS MADE BY MANOLO AT J.F.K.

Manolo was not uniformly successful at J.F.K.. Whereas at Garden School he had been the best student in his original NEP group, at J.F.K. he was competing with peers whose parents were college graduates and professionals. In some classes, Manolo did well. His science teacher, for example, thought highly of him and considered him to be doing average work. His math teacher, on the other hand, immediately became concerned about Manolo and even asked me if he was disabled in his own language. In her math class, Manolo appeared uninterested and distracted and seemed unable to engage in problem-solving activities or in writing solutions to the problems of the week. I suspected that neither Mrs. Jackson's sheltered math class nor his previous work in Mexico had prepared him for pre-algebra.

The creative writing teacher was more tolerant. Even though she had not worked with limited-English-speaking students, she expected that Manolo could develop his own voice. She shared with us the following writing assignment (an essay on Mexican historical figures), which she graded as acceptable.

"*A War*"
The war was between Mexico and France, France was wining they were getting closer to the castle of getting. On the top of the castle the Mexican flag was still flying. If the French soliders pulled the falg down and raise up their own Mexico would be declared a part of France. As the French soldiers got closer to the castle, there were less people protecting the Mexican fort, in the castle were the kid heroes they were cadets from the army of Mexico. The oldest one was 16

the others were from 16 to 10. Most the the kid heroes died protecting the castle.

"They give their lives for their country."

The French soliders got in to the castle there were three kid heroes left, and some soldiers still protecting the castle the others got kill, the three kids that were left run to the top of the castle two died right on the top the one who was left got shoot he took the flag down put it around his body and he jump down the castle when he hit the ground he died. When the French soldiers found the flag and the kid they could not take over Mexico because the flag had blood on it Mexico had won the war.

The teacher seemed a bit baffled about this text. She did not quite understand what Manolo had tried to do. She had, nevertheless, responded to it and asked questions about meaning. She had not corrected his grammar or his punctuation. She was aware that she should not discourage Manolo's early writing attempts.

For us, Manolo's text was full of meaning. In it, he had tried to recount the tale of the *Niños héroes de Chapultepec* (the Boy Heroes of Chapultepec), known to every schoolchild in Mexico. However, since Manolo had little sense of what his readers might need to know to make sense of his recounting, he provided no explanations that might have helped his teacher's understanding.

The text does show that Manolo was able to write longer segments of connected discourse to narrate and recount a historical event. Oral style, however, is still quite present, as is transfer from Spanish. Moreover, punctuation is nonexistent.

The creative writing teacher did not give up on Manolo. She encouraged him to find whatever might interest him to write about, and she responded to his writing as a sympathetic and interested reader. She was delighted when Manolo published a "book" that was bound and displayed in the classroom.[1]

PROGRESS AT THE END OF 2 YEARS

Although I was not able to assess Manolo's English formally, the rate of development of his writing abilities over a 2-year period indicated that he had made excellent progress in English. His texts contained what some teachers might consider many flaws and many errors in idiomatic usage as well as what some researchers might consider evidence the Manolo had created an interlanguage that was systematic and rule-governed. But compared to where he had been a year before, Manolo was moving steadily forward in acquiring English.

It is important to note, however, that at J.F.K. Manolo was not one of the best and the brightest. He was one of the few Mexican students in the school, and he did not have the advantages of many of his peers. Baffled by the tremendous jump that his math class took, for example, he lost confidence in his abilities. His English was not the problem. He simply did not have the appropriate background for the level of the class.

Overall, at J.F.K. Manolo's problem was not language. It involved being 13, having received a very mediocre education in Mexico, and having developed minimal study habits. It also involved being in a new school, having to make new friends, and discovering that he was not quite as good as he had thought himself to be at Garden.

7

Bernardo

Bernardo was a very serious and quiet youngster of 13 who appeared to be almost a full-blooded Mexican Indian. He had very dark skin, high cheekbones, and slightly slanted eyes. He and his 15-year-old sister Marica entered Garden Middle School in January. They had been in Mission Vista for a number of months but had not attended school because their mother could not produce a birth certificate for them. When certificates were finally sent from Mexico, their father, Arnoldo Salas, enrolled them in school.

Like the other fathers, Arnoldo had been in the United States for a number of years. He had worked mainly in restaurants but had also done yardwork, light construction, and odd jobs. His wife, Petra, had come to this country first. After she had given birth to a child here, the couple sent for their two older children. The baby was 18 months old at the start of the study. In Mexico, Marica had completed the third year of *secundaria* and Bernardo had completed the first year. It appeared that the Salas family—unlike many families in Mexico—had not needed their children in the labor force but had been able to afford to keep them in school.

Like the Duque family, the Salas family lived in the more run-down part of the immigrant sector of Mission Vista. They, too, lived in an old apartment building that had peeling paint, a yard littered with trash, and a swimming pool that had been boarded over with large pieces of plywood. The family lived on the second floor, in a two-bedroom apartment, and shared their space with another couple and their child.

Mr. Salas had the same coloring as Bernardo, a very warm and positive attitude, and a sense that things could be done here much the way they had been done in Mexico. For example, when Petra started work in the food service department of a large local university, Bernardo was expected to walk several miles to the campus to escort his mother home after work. This was considered much more important than doing homework or participating in after-school activities. The expectation was that, in the absence of his father, Bernardo would take on the role of the protector of his mother and sisters. Petra commented that Arnoldo believed strongly that boys should learn to be responsible for their families.

Both Petra and Arnoldo knew very little about American schools. School, however, was important to them. They had little to say about why it was important or what they expected from schools. However, when asked directly, Petra responded that it was important for young people to study "para que se realicen" (so that they could be all that they could be).

In general, Petra and Arnoldo were eager to believe that schools were better here than they had been in Mexico and that their children would learn more. Like Mrs. Fuentes, Arnoldo had a very low opinion of Mexican teachers, primarily because of his own experience in schools.

In Mexico, Bernardo had followed the normal demanding curriculum of a federal *secundaria* (middle school), taking Spanish (language arts), math, natural sciences, physical sciences, English, physical education, and art. His study of English appears to have been typical of foreign-language classes in which the primary focus is grammar and vocabulary. Bernardo commented that he had learned very little English, although he had made good grades. He also commented that he worked hard at school and that he had received a medal of distinction in his first year of *secundaria*.

IN THE CLASSROOM

At Garden School, everything was different for Bernardo. There were no challenging subjects to study, and there was little hard work to be done. Bernardo sat quietly and attended to the work he had been given. From time to time, he would look up at his sister Marica for a confirming nod or shake of the head. During most of the first year, he worked on an endless number of worksheets. He was never called on during class by the teacher, and he was seldom called on in small-group work with Mrs. Ayub. He seldom spoke to students around him. He did not participate in the repetition exercises conducted by Mrs. Ayub, in correcting the sentences on the board, or in hang-the-spider. Bernardo carefully copied whatever was on the board, and worked diligently to produce the guided compositions that Mrs. Gordon assigned.

Mrs. Gordon could say little about Bernardo. Since he had entered in January, she assumed that he would be in NEP class again the following year. Bernardo, however, looked sad. He had brought all his books with him from Mexico, and he had expected to study hard. At Garden, the days seemed long and the work, tedious. By February, he was ready to leave school. He told us that he had tried to persuade his father to let him go to work instead. His father had refused because his boss had told him that in this country, youngsters had to stay in school until they were 16.

STARTING OUT

Because Bernardo had entered Garden School in January, we first assessed his academic Spanish levels and his English-language proficiency at that time. Even though he was newly arrived, we used the English-language procedures used in assessment II for the other focal students. These procedures included a number of English-language academic tasks.

Reading and Writing in Spanish

For the Spanish reading segment of the assessment, Bernardo selected a Spanish-language newspaper from our selection and read silently. He summarized the content of the news article in a few sentences and was able to respond to my additional questions on the piece. He read rapidly and competently and demonstrated comprehension of small subtleties in the article.

Bernardo's writing in Spanish was much more extensive than that of the other three focal students. In response to our request that he write about himself, Bernardo wrote the following text, which is laid out exactly as he wrote it.

1.—Yo naci en el Hospital De Toluca
2.—fui creciendo cunpliendo los 6 años
me metieron a la Escula de Cuauchilés
La escuela era muy bonita cegido ponian
Árbolitos ponian plantas de fruta pero
Los niños les decian alas Maestras
que no pusieran por que los niños
que estudian en la tarde en la escuela
los maltratan los quitan.
Los maestros hacen grupos paraque un dia
los riege uno cada quien tiene su dia para
regalos. Mi pápa ce hiva a venir para a ca
pero yo no queria y siempre ce vino
des pues pasaron los 9 meces y mi máma
ce alivio de mihermanita y yo estaba en
la escuela Despues mi hermanina
pasaron 8 meses y mi pápa ce trajo a

mi máma y pasando los meses
Al Año con 7 meses nos mando atraer mi
pápa y mi máma a mi hermana y ami

[1.—I was born in the Hospital in Toluca.
2.—I grew and when I turned six
they put me in the Cuauchilés school
The school was very pretty often they planted
little trees they planted fruit plants but
the children would tell the teachers
not to plant them because the children
that went to school in the afternoon
damaged them and pulled them out.
The teachers form groups so that one day
one waters them each one has a day
to water them. My father was going to come here
but I did not want him to and he came anyway
after those 9 months went by and my mother
had my little sister and I was
in school After my little sister
8 months went by and my father brought
my mother over and as the months passed
At a year and 7 months my father and my mother,
sent for my sister and me]

Bernardo's writing was characterized by a number of spelling confusions that are quite typical of Spanish-speaking individuals who have not received much education. These confusions include the use of the grapheme *c* to spell the sound [s] (e.g., *ce vino* for *se vino*), the overuse of the grapheme *h*, which is silent in Spanish (as in *hiva* for *iba*); and the use of the grapheme *v* for *b*. The presence of such features in Bernardo's text reflects the fact that his experience in writing original texts was probably limited. According to Bernardo, "writing" assignments at his school mainly involved copying texts verbatim.

Bernardo produced a total of eight segments that were complete sentences but used only two periods and five capitals in sentence-initial positions. He did not use commas or other punctuation marks and had many more misspellings in addition to the spelling confusions mentioned above.

In terms of content, Bernardo did indeed provide some of the information expected in a piece of writing focusing on himself. However, at first glance, the text appears to deal with two completely different topics: (1) a description of his school and the trees planted at the school and (2) a narrative about when the family came to the United States. A more detailed examination of the piece suggests that he might have attempted to write an account of his coming to the United States that began with a description of the setting for his narrative (his school in Mexico) and moved from there to describe the events that led to the family's migration. His attempt was unsuccessful. Transitions are missing between events, and the ending is undeveloped. The attempt itself is revealing, however. Bernardo tried to write more than a simple description of himself. By describing his school, he attempted to provide a frame of reference within which his experience and his feelings about moving to a new country might be understood. In comparison to the papers produced by the other focal students, Bernardo's piece was the most ambitious.

Beginning English-Language Abilities

As expected, Bernardo's proficiency in English was indeed close to zero. He could respond at the one-word level but struggled to use context to assign meaning to words and phrases. The following transcribed segments reflect these limitations.

Interviewer: OK. What is your name?
Bernardo: Bernardo Salas. *(Understands/responds)*
Interviewer: Aha, nice to meet you, Bernardo. Where do you live?
Bernardo: Uhm. (*silence*) *(Fails to understand)*
Interviewer: OK. What is your telephone number?
Bernardo: 9–6–1–15–10. *(Understands/responds)*
Interviewer: Good. Where were you born?
Bernardo: (*silence*) No. *(Fails to understand)*
Interviewer: No. How old are you?
Bernardo: Uhm. es bien no. *(Fails to understand)*
Interviewer: Sí, y este how old are you? Twelve, thirteen, fourteen?
Bernardo: Ah este, uhm, thirteen. *(Understands with help)*
Interviewer: Thirteen. OK, good. What is your nationality? What country are you from?
Bernardo: Linden. [Gives street name] *(Fails to understand)*
Interviewer: What school do you go to?
Bernardo: Garden Middle School. *(Understands/responds)*
Interviewer: Garden Middle School. Good. What grade are you in?
Bernardo: (*silence*) No *(Fails to understand)*

Quite surprisingly, however, given what appeared to be a limited understanding of routine personal information questions, Bernardo was able to understand a segment of academic discourse and to use real-world knowledge to guide his understanding. As will be recalled, the academic listening comprehension activity for assessment II included a presentation about Hawaii. Students were asked to recall three things that they learned from the presentation.

Bernardo was unable to use English to demonstrate understanding of the information he had received about Hawaii. However, using Spanish, he recalled the three facts that he had been directed to remember. His presentation of these facts is included below with an English translation following.

> *Interviewer:* Dime, qué tanto me entendiste de lo que dije de
>   Hawaii?
> [Tell me, how much did you understand of what I told you about
>   Hawaii?]
> *Bernardo:* De Hawaii queda de los Estados Unidos. (*Pointing to the
>   map in front of him*) Que son nueve islas. Nueve, como son, si.
> [About Hawaii it's located from the United States. (*pointing to the
>   map in front of him*) That here are nine islands, nine, they are,
>   yes.]
> *Interviewer:* Islas.
> [Islands.]
> *Bernardo:* Si.
> [Yes.]
> *Interviewer:* Y—
> [And—]
> *Bernardo:* Y aquí Estados Unidos, city.
> [And here the United States, city.]

While encouraging, Bernardo's ability to talk about Hawaii may have had less to do with his understanding of the English-language presentation than with his existing knowledge of Hawaii and of geography in general.

For his reading in English, Bernardo selected a selection on Pelé from an ESL reader about famous people. With the passage in front of him. Bernardo wrote the following summary of the selection.

pele have friends   played soccer
pele he played for the New York   Pele
played his first   Pele He became a
millionaire   He was the most famous

As will be noted, Bernardo appeared to be copying directly from the text, and in one instance, it is possible that he did not understand exactly what he was copying. This is suggested by the fact that he left the sentence "Pele played his first" unfinished.

Bernardo's limitations were far more evident, however, on the writing task in which he was asked to write about his school or his family. For this task, Bernardo wrote:

fader eat the beibi have pencil sister

Like Lilian and Elisa, Bernardo merely provided a list of English words. He, too, had very limited English proficiency in both the oral and the written modes. Unlike the other three students, however, Bernardo had a very strong academic background in Spanish. With instruction in English designed to capitalize on these strengths, he could have made rapid progress.

ACCESS TO ENGLISH AT SCHOOL

Like the other focal students, Bernardo had very limited access in school to English-speaking peers. He was enrolled in the NEP core for three periods, in sheltered math with Mrs. Jackson, in sheltered science with Mrs. Morton, in sheltered computers with Mrs. Thompson, and in PE. During breaks and at lunchtime, Bernardo sat with his sister and with a group of other students who lived in the same apartment complex.

SHELTERED CLASSES

Like Elisa, Bernardo was enrolled in Mrs. Jackson's sheltered math class. During class, Bernardo would sit quietly near the back of the room and, as usual, say nothing. When called on to work a problem on the board, he would do so quickly without attending to comments made by the class comedians. When we asked how he liked the class, he admitted that it was too easy because he had studied what they were covering in Mexico.

Bernardo's favorite class was sheltered computers. It was taught by Dorothy Thompson, a very experienced teacher, who used her corpulent presence, her authoritative voice, and her smattering of Spanish to teach students how to work with ancient Apple II computers in her NEP computer class. She normally attached an overhead display to a computer and demonstrated how students should work with particular software programs. Mrs. Thompson frequently shouted over the hum of the students' voices, used Spanish commands, and walked around to see what students were doing. Two NEP students shared each of the 20 Apple II computers in the lab.

During the year, Mrs. Thompson taught students how to use the program *Timeline* and required them to produce a timeline of their lives, beginning with the year they were born and continuing with when they started to read, when they started school, and so on. Students first wrote in Spanish and then had someone help them translate the events into English in order to enter them into the computer.

Most students eagerly sat at the computers and waited for their turn. They appeared not to mind old and malfunctioning equipment: 5¼ floppy disks and two very slow printers. Bernardo proudly showed us his completed timeline, which he explained needed 20 feet to be extended completely.

For Dorothy Thompson, teaching sheltered computers was important because it offered ELL students an opportunity to do something that was highly valued in the world around them. She did not want them to be left out. Students were eager to learn and excited about working with the machines, and they made every attempt to communicate with her in a combination of telegraphic English and telegraphic Spanish.

ENGLISH AT THE END OF THE FIRST YEAR

As was expected, Bernardo's performance on the end-of-year assessment was quite poor. After 5 months of exposure to English, his knowledge of this language was still quite limited. The following transcribed segments reflect these limitations:

Interviewer: OK, Bernardo, how are you?
Bernardo: Good   *(Understands/responds)*
Interviewer: Where do you hear English?
Bernardo: *(No answer)*   *(Fails to understand)*
Interviewer: Do your brothers and sisters
    speak English? Do your mother and fa-
    ther speak English? You don't hear it at
    home. Do you watch TV in English.
Bernardo: No.   *(Understands/responds)*
Interviewer: Tell me who in your family
    speaks English?
Bernardo: My . . . uncle.   *(Understands/responds)*

For the writing assessment, Bernardo produced the following text:

Bernardo
Mi name is Bernardo Salas have
13 I'm lake play soccer.
Mi love fathe, mothe, sisters
counsin and uncle.

As will be noted, he had made some progress in writing in English. He attempted to give information about his family by writing simple unconnected segments that he could probably produce orally. His writing reflects transfer from Spanish, and his spelling errors are frequent. He does not attend to capitalization and punctuation.

THE SECOND YEAR AT GARDEN MIDDLE SCHOOL

At the beginning of the second year, Bernardo was once again placed in the NEP core, having received a grade equivalent score of 1.4. on the Gates-MacGinitie Reading Test. Because of his very low score, Bernardo's placement was straightforward. He remained in the NEP class for the entire year.

Bernardo began the school year with the schedule shown in Table 7.1. Like Elisa, Bernardo was placed in Mrs. Gordon's class and in sheltered classes in science, social studies, and home arts. Surprisingly, in spite of his very serious limitations in English, he was placed in a math class that primarily enrolled mainstream students. Although he experienced serious difficulties, he remained in this class for the greater part of the year. I conjec-

Table 7.1. Bernardo's Schedule

Period	Classes
1	NEP sheltered social studies 6–8
2	NEP core
3	NEP core
4	Math (advanced) 7
5	NEP sheltered science
6	NEP home arts
7	PE 7–8

ture that students such as Bernardo were placed in the lowest-level mainstream math class because of the increasing number of ELL students entering the school. Bernardo's math skills were not assessed before he was placed in the mainstream math class.

For Bernardo, his mainstream math class was frustrating and discouraging. In class, he appeared to be attempting to use his previous knowledge of math to survive, but he became more discouraged as time went on. He did not understand the teacher's presentations, the explanations and instructions in his textbook, or the word problems that he was expected to solve.

The following transcript captures the difference between the language produced in the math class and that heard by Bernardo in his NEP core and sheltered classes.

Teacher: There are two types of fractions. Proper fractions. Proper. That is a proper fraction. The number on top is smaller. The number on the bottom is bigger. That's called a proper fraction. Improper fraction.

(*Interrupts to address students*) Will you all kind of hold on and hold all of your thoughts, then I don't have to . . . Juan. You won't understand this if you don't pay attention.

(*Continues*) Improper fractions. Number on top is bigger than the number on the bottom. OK. Now, when the number on the top—

(*Responding to a student's comment*) I know you know, but just kind of hang on to your thoughts. Let's just review for a second. Joel, page 38. Try to pay attention because this is very important.

Number on top is bigger than the number on the bottom. Improper. Improper fractions can be changed to what is called a mixed number. You can get the mixed number by dividing the top number by the bottom number (*writes on board*). 5 divided by 2. 2; ½ left over.

That's called a mixed number.

Yesterday we started multiplying whole numbers by fractions; like this here. (*writes*) 5 times 1/9th. We found that we put the whole number over a 1 and you just multiply. We saw in the picture that if you have 1/9th and you had five of those ⅑ths, you had ⅝ths. The bottom number is called the denominator. This one (*pointing to the top number*) is called the numerator. Now you multiply a mixed number by a fraction. Do we know how to multiply a fraction by a fraction? But how do you multiply a mixed number by a fraction?

Student 1: First you add the denominators right?
Teacher: No.
Student 2: First you make the one and a half a mixed number.
Teacher: Not a mixed number; it already is a mixed number.
Student 3: You go for a common denominator
Teacher: Not yet, no, that's adding and subtracting.
(Many students begin to call out answers)
Teacher: OK. You have to change the mixed number back into a
   fraction. Now you do that real simple. You change 2 and ½,
   which is a mixed number, back into an improper fraction. You
   multiply 2 times 2 is 4 plus 1 is five halves. So you can change an
   improper fraction to a mixed number or a mixed number to an
   improper fraction. Got it? So we have 1½ times ⅓. We're going
   to change the mixed number into an improper fraction by multiplying 2 times 1 is 2 plus 1 is 3/2 times. Well, if you think, what is
   1 and a half, it's actually three halves, isn't it? So 1 and ½ is really three halves. What I want you to do is to get out a sheet of
   paper *(Students begin to move around and talk; he stops talking)*
   All right, so remember when we do these exercises. You start, not
   at the oral exercises you start here. Everybody got that. Let's try
   number 2. Let's do a couple of these together.

In this particular example, the teacher explained concepts in English and assumed that all the students could follow his explanation. He spoke rapidly and shifted between calling on students, answering students' questions, and explaining different aspects of the same concept.

For non-English-speaking students, such classroom explanations present many challenges, especially if they do not have a strong background in the subject matter in question. Had Bernardo already mastered improper fractions, he would have been able to follow the English presentation with little difficulty. Unfortunately, Bernardo felt very unsure of his previous knowledge of fractions; therefore, in order to comprehend academic English as used in this particular explanation, Bernardo needed to have been taught how to process such language. He would have needed direct instruction that would have taught him how to:

- Continue to listen (resisting distractions—going past fatigue)
- Guess intelligently at meaning from all cues available
- Listen for known elements (words, phrases)

- Listen for cues within the discourse
- Listen for summary statements
- Attend to essential information
- Listen for gist
- Listen for particular details

Unfortunately, Bernardo had not received such instruction in his ESL classes. As was pointed out earlier, beginning ESL students in Mrs. Gordon's class for the most part worked with vocabulary cards and studied isolated words or filled out worksheets at their tables. Bernardo therefore had no experience in processing rapid explanations intended for fluent native speakers.

By comparison, Bernardo appeared to be quite comfortable in his sheltered NEP science class. It was taught by a teacher who was very experienced in using this approach, and classroom language made fewer demands on students' ability to process language in real time. As will be noted in the sample included below, the teacher was aware of the language limitations of her students and therefore adjusted her own language. She repeated, rephrased, used pictures to illustrate meaning, and drew from students' background knowledge in order to teach new concepts.

Teacher: First I want you to look at the pictures. Don't worry about the words. I want you to look at the picture. This is where I want you to look. I want you to look at this part. This whole thing. We're going to talk about this part. Is this the outside or the inside?

Students: Inside.

Teacher: Inside, OK. This is the inside of something; we have a word for that.
In the middle. How many of you have eaten an apple? I don't know if you know this word or not, but when you eat a whole apple—some might know this word—when you eat, eat, eat the apple. OK you bite and eat the apple. Finally when you finish, you have this in the middle. (*She's drawing the picture on the overhead.*) OK, you don't want to eat this part. This part we throw out.
Does anybody know what we call that part that's in the middle? You might. Somebody might know. Sara, what do you call that?
"Core."
Yes, we call this part of the apple the core. It's in the middle. How many have heard of the word *core*?

OK. If you have not heard, this is what we call a core. A core, apple core. What's apple in Spanish? (*Students call out "manzana."*) Is there a word for core? (*Students call out "corazon."*) Do you have a word for the part in the middle?

OK, well in English we have a word for the middle part, we call it the core. Now when we think of the earth this whole part, this whole thing, not just this little one including the bigger one, this whole part; we call that core. We call that the core.

Now, do you know what ice cream is? (*Students call out "yes."*) Have you all had an ice cream? OK, have you eaten ice cream in a scoop so it's round? Ice cream, like in a cup, and we put a round scoop of ice cream. (*Draws on board.*) Now, ice cream is round and if you put it on the table and you don't eat it right away, what happens? The ice cream melts. OK, the outside will start to melt. The outside will go like this. (*Draws and simulates melting.*) But the inside still hard? The inside is hard but the outside is (*students fill in: melting*). Soft. Kind of like water now. Okay, now this whole part is like an ice cream, but the outside part melting. Kind of like water. It's melting, but the inside it is hard. This is the core and this part in the middle is the ice-cream that's hard. This part is the ice cream that is melting.

So the core has two parts. The core has two parts. (*Student calls out the two parts.*) Right. Very good, Jesus. The inside is hard, right here, because it's not melted. But the outside is melted. So like ice cream, this is all melted but this part in the middle is hard. OK, not melted. Now you look. So this is melted, melted.

As will be noted, the language used by the science teacher tended to repeat more and to use shorter utterances before pausing. She also maintained eye contact with students and attempted to build on their previous knowledge.

In spite of his very obvious discomfort and failing grades, Bernardo's schedule was not changed until quite late in the academic year. He was moved out of the mainstream math class—in the third week of March—and put into another mainstream math class with another teacher.

ENGLISH AT THE END OF THE SECOND YEAR

The results of assessments III and IV revealed that Bernardo's English-language abilities had continued to improve slowly. Even though his produc-

tive abilities continued to be limited—even in answering personal information questions—his receptive abilities showed marked improvement.

Bernardo was able to give a Spanish summary of each of the listening
comprehension passages that he was presented with. His Spanish summaries were brief, however, and he selected only a few key details to recall and
recount. There were other details that he did not attend to and did not
recall even when questioned.

Bernardo could, however, name colors, count by 10s, and write figures
for numbers dictated to him. He could also name the days of the week and
the months as well as objects seen in the classroom. He had trouble naming
objects found in his home but was quite successful in working with the
English-language reading texts presented to him. He responded to questions about the weather included in the passage and summarized key ideas
in the text, stating, for example, that the polar regions were cold and the
tropical regions, hot. He also understood and stated that different climates
cause people to work in different ways.

Bernardo also read quickly through the English-language word problems presented in the math text given to him and was able to determine
what operation was needed in order to find the solution. Even though the
materials used to test students' ability to read math texts were quite simple
and involved only addition and subtraction, it was evident that Bernardo
felt quite comfortable in working with these particular math problems in
English.

The following writing sample was obtained from Bernardo as part of
assessment IV:

> My name is Bernardo. I like play
> soccer I have 14 yers Hold from Mixico city
> I like swiming I have hair black
> leg bit My skin is ~~branu~~ braunw
> I like the movie vethoven and the movie
> colors my father I have

As will be noted, Bernardo included much more information about himself
in this sample than he had in his previous writing.

As was the case with Elisa, we were able to collect a number of written
texts that Bernardo had worked on over the course of the academic year.[1]
In the second semester of the second year (January to May 1993), the
teacher began work on a "long" autobiographical piece. For this piece, the
teacher had introduced a prewriting activity involving semantic mapping.
She handed out blank maps to all students and then proceeded to help
them fill out the various categories. Bernardo's map is shown in Figure 7.1.

Figure 7.1. Bernardo's Conceptual Map

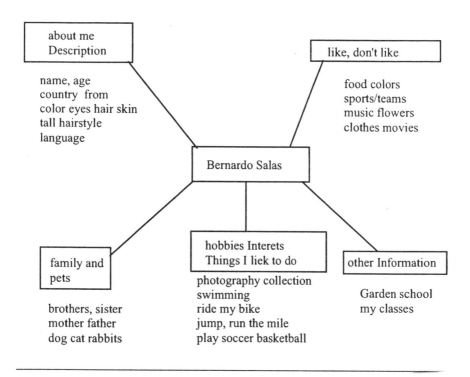

Again, the teacher wrote vocabulary words on the board that students could copy to fill in their various categories. As will be apparent, some of the suggested subcategories made assumptions about the students' lives that were somewhat questionable and revealed the teacher's lack of familiarity with the lives of her students. In our experience, new immigrant students who live in poverty do not have either pets or hobbies.

Once again, even when using a process approach to writing, the teacher did not entirely trust her students to create or communicate their own meanings. The final draft of the piece produced by Bernardo is included below:

My name is Bernardo Salas.
I am 14 year old my color
of my eyes are brown my leg is long
my skin is brown my hair is

black and white my favorite is
language I like play soccer my
favorite color is green, red, blue I like
the jump, run the mile my favorite
teams is raiders. Do you like sports
What team did you like on football.
Do you like raiders. I like chicago bulls
on basketball. In Garden middle school
we have 36 rooms. We don't cat
in the classes I like the movies universal
soulder, vethoven, and the movie Delta
force I have two I like swimming with
my ancles, my father, friends every day my play
soccer in the school Cedars with Daniel,
 Jose.m., Juan. E. Jesus landa and Alfredo my
food favorite is pizza of chese I have
my bike of color black and white
the school garden is big have
cafeteria, library
                    Sencerely
                    Bernardo Salas

At this point in Bernardo's L2 development, he was able to write about
a variety of the categories included on his semantic map. It is evident, however, that he was not writing completely independently. Nevertheless, he
was indeed able to include genuine information about himself, his activities, and his friends. Even though he was confused about the format of the
assignment and even though he included some letter-like elements, it was
Bernardo's first attempt to say something real in writing. With a bit of
effort, the reader of this piece is able to learn that Bernardo is a sports
enthusiast. He appears to be familiar with several teams, and he reports
that he plays soccer with a group of friends, whom he lists.

The piece is not well organized. Bernardo has little notion of paragraph
development or paragraph unity. This is not surprising, because neither
Bernardo nor his classmates received instruction about these matters. Until
this assignment was presented, students had been writing lists of numbered
sentences on a single topic.

Overall, Bernardo's writing development moved slowly. At the end of
the 2-year period in which he had been enrolled primarily in ESL core
(three periods) and in art, cooking, and PE, Bernardo had reached only a
very beginning level of writing proficiency. He could, for example, (1) write
simple unconnected sentences that he could produce orally, (2) write very

short connected discourse on topics about which he could produce connected oral discourse (e.g., family, self, school), and (3) imitate some elements of models of written language presented to him. He often failed, however, to attend to capitalization and punctuation and other details that were included in the models.

LOOKING TOWARD THE FUTURE

As his seventh-grade year ended, there was no doubt in my mind that Bernardo would remain in the NEP or LEP core the following year. I hoped that he would, at least, be placed in the LEP class with Mrs. Clayton so that he might be exposed to a different curriculum. I had many doubts about his being placed in mainstream classes without good instruction in English-language reading and in listening comprehension.

To me, Bernardo was a very sad case. His good academic background in Spanish had not worked to his advantage. He was not able to transfer his well-developed Spanish reading skills to English. He was not taught strategies that might have helped him become a skilled reader of English. Moreover, in the NEP classroom, he had very little access to the kinds of English that he would hear in regular mainstream classrooms. Worst of all, even his sheltered science class gave him only very limited access to the seventh- and eighth-grade science curriculum. He had little opportunity to become excited about learning or to ask questions about how things worked.

Outside of school, Bernardo lived in a Spanish-speaking world. There were no English speakers in his neighborhood, and there were no English speakers in the kitchen of the restaurant where he worked after school with his father. Bernardo was seen as dependable and competent by members of his family. He worked hard on Saturdays, cleaning and hauling and mowing lawns. He contributed to the household and took pride in becoming like his father: a strong and reliable provider for his family. At school, on the other hand, Bernardo enjoyed very little respect. He was seen as incompetent and limited, and no one expected much from him. He was in school because it was important to his father, but Bernardo himself had no illusions. He already knew that he had failed.

8

Learning and Not Learning English

Today, a number of years after the study began, a lot has happened in the lives of Lilian, Elisa, Manolo, Bernardo, and their families. Sonia, Lilian's mother, still cleans houses, but the family has moved to another part of town, away from the intense gang activity. They have purchased a small house, and the family now includes Lilian's older sister, her 3-year old child, Lilian and her children, the older brother, the twins, and the little sister.

Lilian did not finish high school. Like Garden Middle School, the high school she attended was carefully divided into two schools. Lilian was in the ESL track, where she once again had several periods of instruction focusing on English vocabulary, English structure, and English reading. Her subject-matter classes were remedial, taught in slow and simplified English, and aimed at students who, like Lilian, had had very little exposure to academic content in the middle years. Lilian was bored, frequently absent, and, although less rebellious, still completely uninterested in school. Her *quinceañera* party (traditionally given to a girl on her fifteenth birthday) was the highlight of her sophomore year. Soon afterwards, she dropped out to live with a 28-year-old man and his family. She considered herself married and often called to tell me about her life. Four years later, the couple separated. She now has a son and a daughter from two different relationships. Her son's father returned to Mexico before the baby was born, but her daughter's father is nearby and still involved in the baby's life.

Lilian is not defeated. The strong fighting spirit is still there. She loves her children and is determined to make it. Her English, though limited, is good enough for her to work in a fast-food restaurant. Attractive and outgoing, she has told me that she has many opportunities to hear English.

Her long-term plans include going back to school and perhaps becoming a beautician.

In comparison to Lilian, Elisa has learned a lot of English. Nevertheless, she has had to struggle to escape what I have come to call the ESL ghetto. Fortunately for Elisa, she is both strong and determined. For example, when the Garden School ESL teacher did not recommend her for mainstream placement at the high school level, Elisa enlisted my help to register her in another area school where her ESL record would not follow her. We were successful, and Elisa entered a college-bound program in which she was considered to be a regular student. After 2 years of high school in the Bay Area, during which she was enrolled entirely in mainstream classes, the family moved to the Miami area, where, once again, she was enrolled exclusively in mainstream classes. While in school, she worked as a cashier and as a baby-sitter and struggled to keep her grades up. During her senior year, she took the ACT and SAT and prepared for college. Two years later, having decided to attend school in California, she moved back to the area, rented a room from a former teacher, and started work at several different jobs, including baby-sitting, tutoring Spanish, and working at a software company. She took the regular English placement test at a local community college, intending to enroll in a few courses at a time. Unfortunately, Elisa was not permitted to register for classes. Apparently, her placement test revealed that she is not really a native English speaker and she was told that, in order to enroll, she would need to take the ESL placement test and register for ESL writing. The tiny flaws in English that did not prevent her from maintaining a C+ average in high school were nevertheless too much for the sensitivities of community college teachers. Elisa was told that she will not be eligible for enrollment in credit-bearing, college-level instruction in the regular English sequence until she finishes the sequence of ESL courses. Not surprisingly, Elisa was devastated by the recommendation.

When Elisa shared her experience with me, I must confess to feeling outraged. Like middle schools and high schools that isolate students in ESL tracks, the community college system appears to have created an ESL sequence whereby the mainstream faculty can once again put non-English-background students in the care of language specialists. It does not matter that these non-English-background students are fluent English speakers who have already demonstrated their ability to do academic work in English. Regular teachers still do not want to be made uncomfortable by these students' slightly flawed English.

Manolo attended high school in the same affluent community where he attended middle school, where he was surrounded by youngsters who were not only expected to excel in school by their successful parents but were rewarded for their achievements with expensive cars and clothes. His

ESL classmates from middle school enrolled in honors math and English, while he was placed in "general" courses intended for "less motivated" students. Manolo took it easy and looked down on "grade-mongers" who, he said, "came unglued" if they received low grades. One of his teachers commented that at school, between classes, he sat with other low-track students and cynically made fun of "preppies" who really tried hard.

According to one of his classmates, after graduating from high school, Manolo worked as a technician for an electronics firm for two years. When the firm downsized and let him go, he seemed discouraged and decided to work in a small grocery store owned by members of his family.

Bernardo was placed in the LEP core during the eighth grade at Garden and then in the ESL track in high school. At Mission Vista High School, he took ESL 2, 3, and 4. He enrolled almost exclusively in sheltered classes (called ESL subject-matter classes) during the entire 4 years. He also enrolled in a few low-level required classes open to all students.

Unlike Lilian, Bernardo did not drop out. He was serious and kept out of trouble. His teachers had little to say about him except that he came to class regularly and that he kept away from gang activity. Bernardo, recalling his high school experience 1 year after graduation, commented that his classmates were childish and irresponsible and that most of the time he learned very little. He is proud of the fact that he held a full-time job during his high school years and that he was able to contribute to the support of his family. He is confident that the English he has learned is enough to allow him to speak to his employers and fellow employees. He has no plans to attend college.

IMPLICATIONS FOR POLICY AND PRACTICE

The school experiences of Lilian, Elisa, Manolo, and Bernardo, their successes and their failures, have much to tell us about the lives that immigrant children live. They also have much to teach us as we debate policies about the design of educational programs, about teacher preparation, about testing, and most importantly about the role of English in the education of newly arrived children.

As the experiences of the four youngsters make evident, moreover, the relationship between teaching and learning a language is not straightforward. During their middle school years, Lilian, Elisa, Manolo, Bernardo, and their classmates were engaged in the process of acquiring English as a second language. This process, rather than being simple and well understood, is considered by researchers to be extraordinarily complex. Equally complex is the question of what kinds of classroom and school conditions can bring about the most rapid and most effective development of a second language.

For non-English-background students, whose future depends on their learning English, how well this teaching is done and how successful schools are in creating a context in which students have access to English during the schoolday will largely determine whether they acquire English at all and whether they receive an education. As we saw in the cases of Lilian, Elisa, Manolo, and Bernardo, in spite of their three-period-a-day ESL class, they had very few opportunities to interact in English with native English speakers. They were completely isolated from English-speaking same-age peers. All interactions in English took place exclusively with the teacher at a ratio of 1 to 30 or 35. The rest of the time, they were engaged in seatwork focused on learning vocabulary or copying sentences. Little went on in the classroom that could prepare them to develop the kinds of proficiencies they would need to succeed in other classes. Teachers' goals and objectives involved following the textbook, teaching English-language forms, and sometimes merely keeping the children quiet.

Placing beginning students in subject-matter classes in which teachers attempted to simplify their English also did not appear to be successful. Newly arrived youngsters who knew no English could not learn science or math because they could not comprehend the language of either the teacher or the textbook. Youngsters who had some background in the subject were overwhelmed by youngsters who knew little or knew nothing.

What is evident from observations of both the NEP core at Garden Middle School and the newcomer program at Crenshaw School is that sequestering English-language learners for all or most of the day to "study" English may not result in the outcomes that the children themselves, their families, and the public are expecting. Contrary to what proponents of Proposition 227 in California have claimed, *English cannot be learned in a single year.* This is especially the case for students who have access to English only at school. Both Elisa and Manolo made more progress than Lilian and Bernardo because they had parents and relatives who spoke English and opportunities to engage in real communicative interactions with fluent speakers. As the transcripts and writing samples I have included here make clear, however, even after *2 years,* both Manolo and Elisa produced English that many teachers would consider seriously flawed.

EFFECTIVE SCHOOLING FOR IMMIGRANT STUDENTS

The challenges faced by Lilian, Elisa, Manolo, and Bernardo suggest that concerns and assumptions currently guiding the planning and implementation of programs for newly arrived immigrant students—especially at the middle school and high school levels—must be reconceptualized and reoriented. As a nation, we know that these children are not doing well in school, and we are disappointed and concerned. We must admit, however, that the challenges of educating children who do not speak English are extremely complex and that there are no single factors, no single villains that can be identified as the primary causes of immigrant children's low achievement. It is especially important that in moments of anti-immigrant sentiment and English-only fervor we remember that the role of schools is not merely to teach English but to educate children, develop their fine minds, and prepare them to contribute to this country's future.

Below I offer a set of recommendations designed to inform both practice and current policy debates about appropriate programs for newly arrived immigrant students. These recommendations are based on the in-depth study of the four focal students described in this book, on the extensive observation of three middle schools over a 2-year period, and on the practices of numerous other schools where I have conducted research during the last decade.

Recommendation 1

ELL students must be offered ESL courses that are designed to develop their academic English, *that is, the English-language skills needed for "unrestricted access to grade-appropriate instruction in challenging academic subjects" (TESOL, 1997, pp. 1–2).*

In mandating English-language courses for immigrant students, policy makers must move beyond the simple assumption that any ESL course is by definition a good course. In order for students to develop the kinds of English-language proficiency required to achieve in school, the focus and primary objective of ESL programs in middle school and high school must be the development of academic language. Explicit attention must be given to developing students' receptive skills in listening and reading as well as to their productive skills in speaking and writing.

As I pointed out in the cases of Lilian and Bernardo, ESL classes in which activities center primarily on language structure and isolated vocabulary will not help students to develop academic language proficiency. Moreover, according to Wong Fillmore (1985), classes in which students are discouraged from talking to one another, where they primarily fill out worksheets, and where the teachers ask only low-level questions answerable with one word will not provide the kind of input that learners need in order to acquire language.

The most effective ESL classes are those that integrate both language and content. In integrated language and content courses, ESL teachers teach content (social studies, mathematics) to English-language learners using specially designed curriculum units that help students to acquire knowledge in the subject matter area while developing English-language skills. What is different is that ESL teachers, not subject-matter teachers, focus on real academic content (e.g., Why do revolutions take place? Do you think games of chance are fair?) and also teach reading skills, vocabulary in context, forms in context, and academic listening skills on the topics covered.[1]

Recommendation 2
Programs for immigrant students must be seen as schoolwide initiatives for which all teachers are responsible.

English-language learners must be seen as the responsibility of all teachers, not as the exclusive concern of ESL teachers. Schoolwide language policies need to be developed (Corson, 1999) in which the language problems present in each school are identified and the solutions to these problems are agreed upon. Ideally a school language policy, according to Corson (p. 61), "sees language as the central instrument in learning and the most accessible language pedagogy available to teachers." In drafting such a policy, the views and wishes of all stakeholders are taken into account (teachers, parents, community members, students) and an action plan is developed that addresses key issues and seeks to remove the causes of disagreement among practitioners. The intent is to have all members of the school community agree about the nature of the problem and the importance of addressing the problem as an entire school.[2]

The teachers at both Garden Middle School and Crenshaw School viewed English-language learners as the property of the ESL and newcomer classes. They saw ELL students as a special problem that needed to be handled by language specialists. The teachers at J.F.K. Middle School, on the other hand, viewed English-language learners as competent students who would enter their classes sometime during the 3 years of middle school. ESL teachers taught both "regular" classes and ESL classes. Moreover, a climate had been created in which all teachers participated in decisions made about ESL students.

Recommendation 3
All school personnel must contribute to creating a context in which English-language learners have access to both interpersonal and academic language.

Research in L2 acquisition has clearly established the importance of access to meaningful language in the acquisition process. Classroom and school contexts must be created in which learners have the opportunity to interact with native speakers of English in both academic and personal exchanges. Creating such a climate will require collaboration among mainstream teachers and teachers considered specialists on immigrant students. ESL and other specially prepared teachers must teach courses that prepare students to succeed in regular mainstream courses. They cannot, by themselves, prepare ELL students to succeed academically. They must, therefore, become informed about the specific linguistic challenges faced by students in different subject-matter classes, including textbook difficulty, demands made by group interactions, and characteristics of the language challenges present in standardized tests. Preteaching vocabulary for particular subjects is not sufficient.

As we saw in the case of Bernardo, the activities in the ESL classroom did not prepare him to understand explanations in his math class during the second year, to read word problems in his textbook, or to ask clarification questions of his teacher.

Recommendation 4
Schools must find ways to end the isolation of immigrant students.

When English learners far outnumber the native speakers who are available to provide them with access to English, these learners will face serious challenges in acquiring both conversational and academic English. According to Wong Fillmore (1992), in such contexts learners have little access to meaningful input and few opportunities to interact with fluent speakers of the language. They are surrounded by speakers of imperfect English who are themselves learners of English. Given their lack of access to native-like English, students may not develop a full mastery of the standard forms of English. As was the case with Lilian and Bernardo, moreover, their acquisition of English may take place very slowly.

Schools must make deliberate efforts to end the isolation of immigrant students within schools. They must find ways of bringing about interaction between mainstream students and newly arrived students in authentic activities and tasks that can promote both goodwill among youngsters and English-language models for new learners. Initially such efforts might be limited to mainstream students who volunteer to be part of a buddy system, who receive service-learning credit as language mentors, or who can participate in two-way language-learning exchanges (Spanish/English). In other schools, such efforts will include grouping students heterogeneously in subject-matter classrooms within which the language strengths of native-speaking students are used as resources for language learners. In such classrooms, as compared to SDAIE classrooms, the responsibility of providing access to both subject matter and language is not seen as exclusively the teacher's. Classroom tasks are planned in which group work provides access to a rich curriculum to both groups of students as well as provides good models of academic language for ELL students.

The importance of ending the isolation of immigrant students can perhaps be best appreciated by recalling that many older immigrants claim to have learned English quickly in the classroom without special support. They often publicly question the need for special programs for today's immigrant students. Interestingly, such individuals rarely mention the ratio of native speakers to English-language learners in their classrooms. They may not know that if native speakers of English far outnumbered English learners in their classrooms, their success may have had less to do with their personal dedication than with the fact they were not isolated from native English speakers. When there are many native speakers in a classroom, learners have access to a language-rich acquisition environment in which the following ideal conditions, specified by Wong Fillmore (1991), are present:

1. learners who realize that they need to learn English and are motivated to do so;
2. speakers of English who know English well enough to provide the learners with access to the language and the help for learning it; and
3. a social setting which brings learners and English speakers into frequent enough contact to make language learning possible. (p. 51)

As we saw in the case of Bernardo and Lilian, motivation is a crucial factor in language acquisition. Isolation creates a climate in which youngsters have few incentives for learning English.

Recommendation 5
Schooling must build on the existing academic strengths of immigrant students.

Like Bernardo, many immigrant students arrive in school with well-developed academic abilities. Even those youngsters who have not been particularly successful, like Elisa and Lilian, have developed skills that can transfer to academic work in English. Schooling for such students must build on their existing strengths. It should not be assumed that only the children of well-educated professionals are well educated. School administrators and practitioners can build on existing academic strengths of immigrant students by taking steps such as the following.

1. Advocating for the creation of a national database of school programs in other countries

Administrators and practitioners must propose that a national database on programs of study in countries from which large numbers of immigrants come to the United States be established. Teachers need information, for example, about what students cover and are tested on in Mexican schools. When students such as Bernardo report that they have studied natural science, it is important for teachers to be able to look up the range of coverage of such classes in specific grades. They should also be able to obtain information about grading systems, grade point averages, and ways in which academic distinction is merited. J.F.K. students often provided their teachers with a synopsis of the classes they had taken in their home countries, a description of the level of difficulty of such classes as compared to classes in this country, and an interpretation of the levels of attainment they had achieved in different subjects. These synopses helped teachers to place students appropriately and to suggest remedial work when necessary. A national database would help teachers obtain similar information about working-class students whose parents might not be able to provide them with similar synopses.

2. Teaching language-learning and metacognitive strategies

In order to help students build on their existing academic strengths, they must be taught language-learning and metacognitive strategies (Cantoni-Harvey, 1987; Chamot & O'Malley, 1987; O'Malley & Chamot, 1990; Oxford, 1989). For example, learners need to be taught how to guess at meaning from key words, initiate conversations, use circumlocutions, repeat and imitate language, skim texts, find main ideas, predict outcomes, rehearse language for presentations, and the like. As will be recalled, after being taught a few strategies, Lilian was able to "read" an English-language text using cognates, headings, and illustrations. Bernardo's experience in his math class would have been very different had he been taught how to continue to listen (resisting distractions—going past fatigue), guess intelligently at meaning from all cues available, listen for known elements (words, phrases), and differentiate between essential and nonessential information.

According to Oxford (1994), strategy training research suggests that L2 strategy training should:

- Be based on student needs
- Be integrated into L2 activities over a long period of time
- Include explanations, handouts, activities, reference materials, and materials for home study

- Be explicit and overt as well as offer opportunities for practice
- Provide strategies transferable to the language demands of other classes

For newly arrived students, strategy training may initially need to be carried out in the students' first language.

3. Demanding ESL textbooks that have L1 support

ESL textbooks and other materials must be provided that include L1 support (glossaries, notes, glosses for common expressions, instructions for exercises). Such texts will communicate to learners that they are seen as competent and intelligent young people who can use their L1 literacy skills to support the study of L2. Such texts will also allow learners to study English by themselves, to review materials presented in class, and to read and learn ahead. In states with large numbers of ELL students, teachers must demand that adoption criteria be changed to make certain that publishers produce ESL textbooks with L1 support for languages that have (1) the largest number of speakers, (2) the greatest number of students who are at risk academically, and (3) a standardized, widely used written form.

Recommendation 6
Students must be given access to the curriculum while they are learning English

Helping students to keep up and catch up with the curriculum continues to be one of the most difficult challenges facing schools. Students should not be allowed to fall behind in subject-matter areas (e.g., mathematics, science) while they are learning English. L1 instruction may be an option in some settings. In others, the use of subject-matter texts in L1 may be appropriate. In still other settings, sheltered/SDAIE instruction may be the best solution.

Access to the curriculum must be provided for (1) students, like Bernardo, who have a good academic background; (2) students, like Manolo, who make great progress in English but who have many weaknesses in subject-matter areas; and (3) students, like Juana, who have had little or no schooling in their home countries. Information gathered about students' previous study of particular subjects may help school personnel determine how best to disentangle content knowledge from English-language acquisition so that they can support or remediate the academic background of these students.

Recommendation 7

Revolving-door policies and practices that release English-language learners from ESL programs in one school only to place them in such programs once again in other schools must be changed.

Like Elisa, who was once again placed in ESL non-credit-bearing courses at the community college level, many ESL students are placed in ESL over and over again during their many years of schooling. Students exit from ESL according to one set of criteria (e.g., language examination, teacher recommendation) at one level or in one district only to be placed in the ESL track once again by another set of criteria (mainstream teacher's recommendation, standardized achievement score) at the next level of schooling. Even though rates of reclassification/redesignation have been used in numerous political battles, particularly against bilingual education, politicians and the public seem unaware of the fact that such reclassification is not permanent. Reclassification figures say nothing about revolving-door policies that reclaim the very same students over and over again.

To my knowledge, revolving-door policies have not been examined by either practitioners or researchers. However, it is clear that such policies exist for a number of reasons. ESL teachers often place reclassified students in their programs because they want to make sure they are ready for mainstream instruction. Mainstream teachers who have not worked with ELL learners, on the other hand, often recommend ESL placement when they see the flawed writing of students such as Manolo or Elisa. Because many mainstream teachers know little about the L2 acquisition process or about interlanguages, they imagine that more instruction in traditional grammar in ESL classes will help students eliminate their errors. Finally, administrators often see ELL students' low standardized scores in reading and language arts as indicative of their need for more ESL instruction as opposed to their need for more instruction in reading, in spelling, and in working with academic language. Low-scoring students are sent back to ESL to carry out more drills on bits and pieces of language. No attempt is made to disentangle the effects of various factors (e.g., language limitations, reading skill development, content knowledge) on test scores.

Revolving-door policies will not change until they are examined closely by both teachers and administrators. Their impact on both the schools themselves and on the students who are once again labeled "not ready" must be understood fully. What must guide the examination of these policies is a deep understanding of the complexity of the process of L2 learning, the nature of interlanguages, and the time that it can take for students to sound (or write) like native speakers.

THE POLITICS OF TEACHING ENGLISH

Setting out a clear and unambiguous set of recommendations for English-language learners is an important first step. However, there is much more to consider in implementing programs designed to teach the English language to immigrant students. In recent years, for example, a number of scholar-practitioners who are part of the ESL and EFL professions (e.g., Bhatt & Martin-Jones, 1992; Corson, 1997; Fairclough, 1989; Kaplan, 1997; Penneycook, 1994; Tollefson, 1991; Wallace, 1992) have attempted to point out to their colleagues around the world that the teaching of English is not neutral. They have argued that the key presumption of the discourse of ESL teaching—that it is possible to just teach language—is untenable because it is impossible to separate English from its many contexts.

Working within the framework of critical pedagogy and critical language awareness, these scholars view schools not as "sites where a neutral body of curricular knowledge is passed on to students," but rather as "cultural and political arenas within which various political, cultural, and social forms are engaged in constant struggle" (Penneycook, 1994, p. 297). Fairclough (1989), for example, points out that that these struggles are often obscured. Individuals of goodwill are not aware that they have become instruments of dominant interests. They are seldom conscious of the fact that power is exercised both through coercion and through consent and that, in many cases, people "consent" to preserving the status quo and to maintaining existing power relationships simply by accepting established practices without question.

In examining the politics of English language teaching, a number of individuals have argued that in both English-speaking and non-English-speaking countries, English is one of the "most powerful means of inclusion into or exclusion from further education, employment or social position" (Penneycook, 1994, p. 14). For immigrants to English-speaking countries, then, access to English becomes essential. Unfortunately, according to Tollefson (1995), many English-language educational programs, such as those aimed at Southeast Asian refugees, frequently offer instruction primarily focused on "survival" English that directly channels such immigrants into low-paying jobs. Similarly, school programs aimed at immigrant students, as we saw in the case of four youngsters, are seldom based on an ethical understanding of how education is related to broader social and cultural relations, even though they may make use of a rhetoric of equality and opportunity and claim to prepare students for academic success.

In spite of the complexity of the problem of school failure for non-mainstream children, those concerned about its remediation have focused on attempting to change particular aspects of the institutional and instructional contexts—as I myself have done in making program recommendations—in the hope that such changes will bring about increased school success. While aware of the structural factors that frame the problem, these researchers and practitioners represent the tension that Carnoy and Levin (1985) have described as existing between "the unequal hierarchies associated with the capitalist workplace" and "the democratic values and expectations associated with equality of access to citizen rights and opportunities" (p. 4).

ESL teachers in schools, therefore, frequently promise what they cannot deliver. They suggest that academic success is possible for large numbers of children who are poor and disadvantaged and who do not have access to the kinds of cultural capital valued by schools. Critiquing the notion of language acquisition as a predominantly psycholinguistic phenomenon, Penneycook (1994), for example, argues that language, rather than being isolated from social, cultural, and educational contexts, is at the center of questions concerning education and inequality. Unfortunately, as Tollefson (1995) has pointed out, most teacher education programs in ESL have focused on second-language acquisition, teaching methods and linguistics without placing these fields in their social, political, and economic contexts. For many scholars (e.g., Tollefson, 1995), applied linguistics and language teaching must undergo a critical self-examination. They argue that central concepts in applied linguistics reflect a particular ideological perspective about power relationships. As a result, English-language educators adopt uncritical positions about the value of English and about the place of ESL teaching in the schooling of language-minority students. They often view language as a formal system for study rather than as something that is located in social action. They do not see that language is always situated within larger discursive frameworks and, as Penneycook (1994) put it, is "part of the cultural and political moments of the day" (p. 34).

From the perspective of theorists working from a critical perspective, ESL classrooms—like all classrooms—are sites of struggle. Auerbach (1995), for example, maintains that if classrooms are seen through an ideological lens, the "dynamics of power and inequality show up in every aspect of classroom life, from physical setting to needs assessment, participant structures, curriculum development, lesson content, materials, instructional processes, discourse patterns, language use and evaluation" (p. 12). Textbooks, for example, often become the curriculum itself; the teacher's goal is to cover the material, not to uncover what students want to say or what is important to them. Problems are seen as residing in students, not in text materials or in the decision made by the teacher to focus on rehearsing correct forms as opposed to generating new meaning and sharing information, opinions, and experiences. Much classroom activity is limited to a focus on the basics, that is, pronunciation of isolated forms, memorization of vocabulary items, and practice of grammatical structures. The mastery of basics is seen as a prerequisite to creative communication, and there is no acknowledgment that forms and expressions rehearsed in class actually inculcate norms and social relations.

Equally important and equally political is the fundamental question of which language to use in the teaching of English. As Auerbach (1993, 1995) has argued, little research has been done on the effects of using English exclusively in ESL contexts. Nevertheless, most practitioners view it as a natural and commonsense practice. Indeed, as Phillipson (1988) points out, the ELT (English-language teaching) profession is currently guided by the tenets adopted at the Commonwealth Conference on the Teaching of English as a Second Language held in Makerere, Uganda, in 1961. Phillipson formulates these tenets as follows:

- English is best taught monolingually
- The ideal teacher of English is a native speaker
- The earlier English is introduced the better the results
- The more English is taught the better the results
- If other languages are used in classroom, the standards of English will drop (p. 349)

Auerbach (1993) further maintains that while there is no evidence that the exclusive use of English results in greater or more complete acquisition, there is significant evidence against the use of English only in the classroom. Citing studies by a number of researchers (D'Annunzio, 1991; Garcia, 1991; Hemmindinger, 1987; Klassen, 1991; Rivera, 1988; Robson, 1982; Shamash, 1990), Auerbach maintains that the exclusive use of English in the classroom results in nonparticipation by students, language shock, dropping out, frustration, and inability to build on existing L1 literacy skills. The use of some of the students' native language in the teaching of ESL, on the other hand, has been found to serve as a natural bridge for overcoming problems of vocabulary, for validating learners' lived experiences, for increasing the level of trust between teachers and students, for making rapid gains in English-language development, for monitoring comprehension, and for obtaining information about the metacognitive aspects of language. Auerbach (1995) concludes by saying:

> Despite the fact that use or prohibition of the L1 is often framed in purely pedagogical terms, clearly it is also an ideological issue. Ironically, often the very people who argue vehemently against the English-Only movement on a

societal level insist on the exclusive use of English at the classroom level. My point here is that they are two sides of the same coin: Insistence on English in the classroom may result in slower acquisition of English, a focus on childlike and disempowering approaches to language instruction, and ultimately a replication of relations of inequality outside the classroom, reproducing a stratum of people who can do only the least skilled and least language/literacy dependent jobs. (p. 27)

Issues surrounding selection standards for ESL teachers have also been examined by a number of scholars. Kaplan (1997), for example, points out that many individuals who are currently working as ESL or EFL teachers have received little or no training. In many areas of the world, the mere fact that they are native speakers of English qualifies them for employment as language instructors. He stresses the fact that "some graduates of training programs have not been taught much, and even some teachers have penetrated the field without any training at all" (p. xx).

TOWARD A CRITICAL PEDAGOGY IN ESL

In imagining the teaching of English for the Elisas, Bernardos, Manolos, and Lilians of the world, I envision a critical pedagogy that, as Simon (1986) has pointed out, does not merely involve helping students to "make it," but rather involves trying to change the ways students understand their lives and the possibilities with which they are presented. Critical language study, according to Fairclough (1992), is "an orientation towards language" that "highlights how language conventions and language practices are invested with power relations and ideological processes which people are often unaware of" (p. 7). It would be important, for example, for Elisa to examine exactly why ESL ghettos exist and to find a voice with which to name the very powerful and real barriers that stand in the way of her dreams.

Penneycook (1994) points out that in order for ESL teachers to move beyond where they are now, they must ask themselves "what sort of vision of society" they are teaching toward (p. 299). Moreover, they must have an ethical understanding of how education is related to broader social and cultural relations. He argues that a critical practice of English-language teaching must begin by critically examining and exploring students' knowledge, histories, and cultures in ways that are both affirming and supportive. Teachers must work to help students develop their own voices—not what has been termed the "babble" of communicative language teaching, but rather voices that are tied to a vision of possibilities. In sum, they must help students to find and create insurgent voices—voices that question the reality that surrounds them.

According to Kaplan (1997, p. xxi), teachers must begin by refusing to use intellectually impoverished materials, to teach syllabuses based on irrelevant assumptions, and to teach in programs that intentionally mislead their clients, promising more than they can possibly deliver. Kaplan's indictment includes a criticism of teachers who do not read, who make no sustained effort to learn, and who do not grasp the place of language in the total curriculum.

FINAL WORDS

The teaching of English to immigrant students, rather than being a straightforward and unproblematic practice, is a contested site in which there is a struggle about the role and the future of immigrants in our society. As Americans, we can decide not to address these larger issues and to proceed with our discussions about how many years to teach English. We can pretend that programs, methodologies, and pedagogies are entirely neutral, and we can refuse to examine ESL ghettos, poor teaching, and the isolation of English-language learners in our educational institutions. Schools like Garden Middle School will continue to be effective in separating the newcomers from the regular students, in keeping them out of trouble, and in helping them to accept their place in society. If what we want, on the other hand, is to develop the full intellectual potential of all our citizens and future citizens, the challenge before us is enormous. We must plan carefully, and we must work quickly. There are many Lilians, Bernardos, Manolos, and Elisas in today's schools who deserve a chance to contribute fully to our society and who still believe that they, too, can be a part of the American dream.

Notes

Introduction

1. In order to protect the confidentiality of all project participants, I have not given the exact dates during which the study took place.

Chapter 1

1. OECD countries include Australia, Austria, Belgium, Canada, Denmark, Finland, France, Germany, Greece, Iceland, Ireland, Italy, Japan, Luxembourg, the Netherlands, New Zealand, Norway, Portugal, Spain, Sweden, Switzerland, Turkey, the United Kingdom, and the United States.

2. While these enrollment statistics are revealing of recent trends, according to Hopstock and Bucaro (1993), estimates of future changes in the ELL population based on present or past conditions are problematic. The number of ELL students will be determined by (1) legal and illegal immigration patterns, (2) birthrates of immigrant and language-minority populations, (3) English proficiency levels of arriving immigrants, (4) definitions of limited English proficiency used, (5) rates of reclassification of ELL children, and (6) school attendance and dropout rates

3. For a discussion and rebuttal of the arguments presented against bilingual education during the Proposition 227 campaign in California, the reader is referred to Krashen (1999)

4. Personal communication from Lily Wong Fillmore, November 1996.

5. I discuss English-only policies in the ESL classroom and their implications more fully in Chapter 8.

Chapter 2

1. I am using the terminology used by the school to talk about English-language learners and their programs. The terms NEP (non-English-proficient), LEP (limited-English-proficient), and FEP (fluent-English-proficient) are no longer used by most researchers. I myself prefer to use far more neutral terms such as *English-language learners* or ELL students.

2. Sheltered content courses are classes in which teachers—who may or may not speak the non-English language(s) spoken by their students—present subject-matter instruction using special strategies. They modify their use of English and provide many illustrations of the concepts they are presenting. Research conducted in California on such classes (e.g., Minicucci & Olson, 1992) has found that in comparison to mainstream classes, sheltered classes provide very sparse coverage of the subject-area content.

3. According to Swerdlik's (1992) review of the third edition of the Gates-MacGinitie Reading Test (GMRT), it is designed to provide a general assessment of reading achievement. The GMRT is a power test that focuses primarily on reading vocabulary and comprehension. It was not designed to assess the reading proficiency of English-language learners. There are thus no suggested cutoff scores for placement in ESL levels contained in the test administration materials.

4. Interestingly, the test was also used to place fluent English speakers who had already been mainstreamed back into the ESL sequence. For such students, a low reading score was seen as a signal of incomplete acquisition of English as opposed to a symptom of reading problems. Such low-ability readers, then, were not offered remedial work in reading. They were once again placed in ESL.

Chapter 5

1. For additional examples and analysis of texts written by Elisa during her first two years, see Valdés (1999) and Valdés and Sanders (1998).

Chapter 6

1. For additional examples and analysis of texts written by Manolo during his first 2 years, see Valdés (1999) and Valdés and Sanders (1998).

Chapter 7

1. For additional examples and analysis of texts written by Bernardo during his first 2 years, see Valdés (1999) and Valdés and Sanders (1998).

Chapter 8

1. For examples of materials currently available for integrating language and content, see the Web site for the Center for Applied Linguistics: http://www.cal/org/pubs/materials.htm#ENGLISH.

2. Examples of various types of school language policies are included in Corson (1999).

References

Adams, K. L., & Brink, D. T. (Eds.). (1990). *Perspectives on official English: The campaign for English as the official language of the USA.* Berlin: Mouton de Gruyter.

Asimov, N. (1998, March 17). Bilingual education interpretations vary. *San Francisco Chronicle,* pp. 1A, 11A.

Auerbach, E. R. (1993). Reexamining English only in the ESL classroom. *TESOL Quarterly, 27*(1), 9–32.

Auerbach, E. R. (1995). The politics of the ESL classroom: Issues of power in pedagogical choices. In J. W. Tollefson (Ed.), *Power and inequality in language education* (pp. 9–33). Cambridge, UK: Cambridge University Press.

August, D., & Hakuta, K. (Eds.). (1997). *Improving schooling for language-minority children: A research agenda.* Washington, DC: National Academy Press.

Baron, D. (1990). *The English-only question.* New Haven, CT: Yale University Press.

Bazeley, M., & Aratani, L. (1998, March 22). English-initiative's Spanish-speaking roots. *San Jose Mercury News,* pp. 1A, 24A, 25A.

Berman, P., McLaughlin, B., McLeod, B., Minicucci, C., Nelson, B., & Woodworth, K. (1995). *School reform and student diversity: Case studies of exemplary practices for LEP students.* Berkeley, CA: National Center for Research on Cultural Diversity and Second Language Learning. BW Associates.

Bhatt, A., & Martin-Jones, M. (1992). Whose resource? Minority language, bilingual learners and language awareness. In N. Fairclough (Ed.), *Critical language awareness* (pp. 285–302). London: Longman.

Bialystok, E., & Hakuta, K. (1994). *In other words.* New York: Basic Books.

Bodnar, J. (1982). Schooling and the Slavic-American family, 1900–1940. In B. J. Weiss (Ed.), *American education and the European immigrant: 1840–1940.* Chicago: University of Illinois Press.

Bokamba, E. G. (1991). French colonial language policies in Africa and their legacies. In D. F. Marshall (Ed.), *Language planning.* Amsterdam: John Benjamins.

Bowles, S., & Gintis, H. (1977). *Schooling in capitalist America.* New York: Basic Books.

Bradby, D. (1992). *Language characteristics and academic achievement: A look at Asian and Hispanic eighth graders in NELS 88.* Washington, DC: U.S. Department of Education.

Cantoni-Harvey, G. (1987). *Content-area language instruction: Approaches and strategies.* Reading MA: Addison-Wesley.

Carnoy, M., & Levin, H. (1985). *Schooling and work in the democratic state.* Stanford: Stanford University Press.

Chamot, A. U. (1992). *Changing instructional needs of language minority students. Third National Research Symposium on LEP Students.* Washington, DC: Department of Education.

Chamot, A. U., & O'Malley, M. (1987). *Learning strategies for problem solving.* Reading, MA: Addison-Wesley.

Churchill, S. (1986). *The education of linguistic and cultural minorities.* San Diego, CA: College Hill Press.

Corson, D. (1997). Social justice in the work of ESL teachers. In W. Eggington & H. Wren (Eds.), *Language policy: Dominant English, pluralist challenges* (pp. 149–163). Amsterdam: John Benjamins.

Corson, D. (1999). *Language policy in schools.* Mahwah, NJ: Erlbaum.

Cortes, C. E. (1986). The education of language minority students: A contextual interaction model. In Bilingual Education Office (Ed.), *Social and cultural factors in schooling language minority students* (pp. 3–33). Los Angeles: Evaluation, Dissemination and Assessment Center, California State University.

Craig, D. (1988). Creole English and education in Jamaica. In C. B. Paulston (Ed.), *International handbook of bilingualism and bilingual education* (pp. 297–312). New York: Greenwood.

Crawford, J. (1992). *Hold your tongue.* Reading, MA: Addison-Wesley.

Daniels, H. A. (Ed.). (1990). *Not only English: Affirming America's multilingual heritage.* Urbana, IL: National Council of Teachers of English.

D'Annunzio, A. (1991). Using bilingual tutors and nondirective approaches in ESL: A follow-up report. *Connections: A Journal of Adult Literacy, 4,* 51–52.

Davis, D., & McDaid, J. (1992). Identifying second-language students' needs: A survey of Vietnamese high school students. *Urban Education, 6,* 217–244.

Dinnerstein, L. (1982). Education and the advancement of American Jews. In B. J. Weiss (Ed.), *American education and the European immigrant: 1840–1940.* Chicago: University of Illinois Press.

Doughty, C. (1998). Acquiring competence in a second language. In H. Byrnes (Ed.), *Learning foreign and second languages* (pp. 128–156). New York: Modern Language Association.

Dua, H. R. (1991). Language planning in India: Problems, approaches and prospects. In D. F. Marshall (Ed.), *Language planning* (pp. 104–133). Amsterdam: John Benjamins.

Ekstrand, L. H. (1981). Theories and facts about early bilingualism in native and migrant children. *Grazer Linguistische Studien, 14,* 24–52.

Ellis, R. (1988). The role of practice in classroom language learning. *Teanga, 8,* 1–25.

Ellis, R. (1990). *Instructed second language acquisition.* London: Blackwell.

Ellis, R. (1992). The classroom context: An acquisition-rich or an acquisition-poor environment? In C. Kramsch & S. McConnell-Ginet (Eds.), *Text and context:*

Cross-disciplinary perspectives on language study (pp. 171–186). Lexington, MA: D.C. Heath.

Faerch, C., & Kasper, G. (1987). Perspectives on language transfer. *Applied Linguistics, 8,* 111–136.

Fagerlind, I., & Saha, L. J. (1989). *Education and national development: A comparative perspective* (2nd ed.). Oxford, UK: Pergamon Press.

Fairclough, N. (1989). *Language and power.* London: Longman.

Fairclough, N. (Ed.). (1992). *Critical language awareness.* London, UK: Longman.

Fass, P. S. (1988). *Outside in: Minorities and the transformation of American education.* Oxford, UK: Oxford University Press.

Fleischman, H. L., & Hopstock, P. J. (1993). *Descriptive study of services to limited English proficient students: Volume I. Summary of findings and conclusions.* Washington, DC: U.S. Department of Education.

Foley, D. E. (1990). *Learning capitalist culture: Deep in the heart of Tejas.* Philadelphia: University of Pennsylvania Press.

Garcia, E. (1991). *Education of linguistically and culturally diverse students: Effective instructional practices.* Santa Cruz, CA: National Center for Research on Cultural Diversity and Second Language Learning.

Garcia, E. E. (in press). Bilingualism and schooling in the United States. *International Journal of the Sociology of Language.*

Gass, S. (1984). A review of interlanguage syntax: Language transfer and language universals. *Language Learning, 34,* 115–132.

Gentile, C. (1992). *Exploring new methods for collecting students' school-based writing: NAEP's 1990 portfolio study.* Washington, DC: National Center for Education Statistics.

Glenn, C. L., & de Jong, E. J. (1996). *Educating immigrant children: Schools and language minorities in twelve nations.* New York: Garland.

Handlin, O. (1973). *The uprooted.* Boston: Little, Brown. (Original work published 1951)

Handlin, O. (1979). *Boston's immigrants.* Cambridge, MA: Belknap Press of Harvard University Press.

Handlin, O. (1982). Education and the European immigrant. In B. J. Weiss (Ed.), *American education and the European immigrant: 1840–1940* (pp. 3–16). Chicago: University of Illinois Press.

Harklau, L. (1994a). ESL versus mainstream classes: Contrasting L2 learning environments. *TESOL Quarterly, 28*(2), 241–272.

Harklau, L. (1994b). Tracking and linguistic minority students: Consequences of ability grouping for second language learners. *Linguistics and Education, 6,* 221–248.

Harklau, L. (1994c). Jumping tracks: How language minority students negotiate evaluations and ability. *Anthropology of Education Quarterly, 25*(3), 347–363.

Harklau, L. (1999). The ESL learning environment in secondary school. In C. J. Faltis & P. M. Wolfe (Eds.), *So much to say: Adolescents, bilingualism, and ESL in the secondary school* (pp. 42–60). New York: Teachers College Press.

Haugen, E. (1969). *The Norwegian language in America*. Bloomington, IN: Indiana University Press.

Hemmindinger, A. (1987). *Two models for using problem-posing and cultural sharing in teaching the Hmong English as a second language and first language literacy*. Unpublished master's thesis, St. Francis Xavier University, Antigonish, Nova Scotia, Canada.

Herriman, M. (1996). Language policy in Australia. In M. Herriman & B. Burnaby (Eds.), *Language policies in English-dominant countries* (pp. 35–61). Clevedon, UK: Multilingual Matters.

Hopstock, P. J., & Bucaro, B. J. (1993). *A review and analysis of estimates of the LEP population*. Arlington, VA: Special Issues Analysis Center Development Associates.

Johnston, M. (1985). *Syntactic and morphological progression in learner English*. Canberra, Australia: Department of Immigration and Ethnic Language Affairs.

Kalantzis, M., Cope, B., & Slade, D. (1989). *Minority languages and dominant culture: Issues of education, assessment and social equity*. London: Falmer.

Kaplan, R. B. (1997). Foreword: Palmam quie meruit ferat. In W. Eggington & H. Wren (Eds.), *Language policy: Dominant English, pluralist challenges* (pp. ix–xxiii). Amsterdam: John Benjamins.

Klassen, C. (1991). Bilingual written language use by low-education Latin American newcomers. In D. Barton & R. Ivanic (Eds.), *Writing in the community* (pp. 38–57). London: Sage.

Kleifgen, J. (1985). Skilled variation in a kindergarten teacher's use of foreigner talk. In S. Gass & C. Madden (Eds.), *Input in second language learning* (pp. 59–68). Rowley, MA: Newbury.

Kohl, H. (1991). *I won't learn from you: The role of assent in learning*. Minneapolis, MN: Milkweed Editions.

Kolde, G. (1988). Language contact and bilingualism in Switzerland. In C. B. Paulston (Ed.), *International handbook of bilingualism and bilingual education* (pp. 515–537). New York: Greenwood.

Krashen, S. (1985). *The input hypothesis*. Oxford, UK: Pergamon.

Krashen, S. D. (1999). *Condemned without a trial: Bogus arguments against bilingual education*. Portsmouth, NH: Heinemann.

LaFontaine, H. (1987). *At risk children and youth: The extra-educational challenges of limited English proficient students*. Washington, DC: Council of Chief State School Officers.

Lambert, R. (Ed.). (1994). *Language planning around the world: Contexts and systemic change*. Washington, DC: National Foreign Language Center.

Larsen-Freeman, D., & Long, M. H. (1991). *An introduction to second language acquisition research*. London: Longman.

Lightbown, P. M. (1983). Exploring relationships between development and instructional sequences in L2 acquisition. In H. Sliger & M. Long (Eds.), *Classroom-oriented research in second language acquisition* (pp. 217–243). Rowley, MA: Newbury.

Lightbown, P. M. (1984). Input and acquisition in second language classrooms. *TESL Canada Journal, 1*(2), 55–67.

Lightbown, P. M. (1992). Getting quality input in second/foreign language classroom. In C. Kramsch & S. McConnell-Ginet (Eds.), *Text and context: Cross-disciplinary perspectives on language study* (pp. 187–197). Lexington, MA: Heath.

Long, M. (1981). Input, interaction and second language acquisition. In H. Winitz (Ed.), *Native language and foreign language acquisition* (pp. 379). New York: New York Academy of Sciences.

Long, M. (1983). Native speaker/non-native speaker conversation in the second language classroom. *Applied Linguistics, 4,* 126–141.

Long, M., & Robinson, P. (1998). Focus on form: Theory, research, and practice. In C. Doughty & J. Williams (Eds.), *Focus on form in classroom second language acquisition* (pp. 15–40). Cambridge, UK: Cambridge University Press.

Lucas, T. (1992). *What have we learned from research on successful secondary programs for LEP students? A synthesis of findings from three studies. Third National Research Symposium on LEP Student Issues.* Washington, DC: Department of Education.

Macias, R., & Kelly, C. (1996). *Summary report of the survey of states' limited English proficient students and available educational programs and services 1994–1995.* Washington, DC: George Washington University.

McArthur, E. K. (1993). *Language characteristics and schooling in the United States, a changing picture: 1979 and 1989.* Washington, DC: U.S. Government Printing Office.

Meisel, J., Clahsen, H., & Pienemann, M. (1981). On determining developmental stages in second language acquisition. *Studies in Second Language Acquisition, 3,* 109–135.

Minicucci, C., & Olsen, L. (1992). *Programs for secondary limited English proficient students: A California study.* Washington, DC: National Clearinghouse for Bilingual Education.

Moss, M., & Puma, M. (1995). *Prospects: The congressionally mandated study of educational growth and opportunity. First year report on language minority and limited English proficient students.* Cambridge, MA: U.S. Department of Education and ABT Associates.

Nemser, W. (1971). Approximative systems of foreign language learners. *International Review of Applied Linguistics, 9,* 115–123.

Olneck, M. R., & Lazerson, M. (1988). The school achievement of immigrant children: 1900–1930. In B. McClellan & W. J. Reese (Eds.), *The social history of education* (pp. 257–286). Urbana: University of Illinois Press.

O'Malley, M. J., & Chamot, A. U. (1990). *Learning strategies in second language acquisition.* London: Cambridge University Press.

Oxford, R. (1994). *Language learning strategies: An update* (ERIC Digest). Washington, DC: ERIC Clearinghouse on Languages and Linguistics.

Oxford, R. L. (1989). *Language learning strategies.* New York: Newbury House.

Paulston, C. B. (1986). Linguistic consequences of ethnicity and nationalism in multilingual settings. In B. Spolsky (Ed.), *Language and education in multilingual settings* (pp. 117–152). San Diego, CA: College Hill Press.

Paulston, C. B. (Ed.). (1988). *International handbook of bilingualism and bilingual education*. New York: Greenwood.

Penneycook, A. (1994). *The cultural politics of English as an international language*. London: Longman.

Perlmann, J. (1988). *Ethnic differences: Schooling and social structure among the Irish, Italians, Jews and Blacks in an American city, 1880–1935*. Cambridge, UK: Cambridge University Press.

Persell, C. H. (1977). *Education and inequality: The roots and results of stratification in America's schools*. New York: Free Press.

Phillipson, R. (1988). Linguicism: Structures and ideologies in linguistic imperialism. In T. Skutnabb-Kangas & J. Cummins (Eds.), *Minority education: From shame to struggle* (pp. 339–358). Clevedon, UK: Multilingual Matters.

Phillipson, R., Rannut, M., & Skutnabb-Kangas, T. (1994). Introduction. In T. Skutnabb-Kangas & R. Phillipson (Eds.), *Linguistic human rights: Overcoming linguistic discrimination* (pp. 1–22). Berlin: Mouton de Gruyter.

Pica, T. (1994). Questions from the language classroom: research perspectives. *TESOL Quarterly, 28*(1), 49–79.

Pienemann, M. (1985). Learnability and syllabus construction. In K. Hyltenstam & M. Pienemann (Eds.), *Modelling and assessing second language acquisition* (pp. 23–75). Clevedon, UK: Multilingual Matters.

Portes, A., & Gran, D. (1991). *Characteristics and performance of high school students in Dade County*. Baltimore, MD: Johns Hopkins University Press.

Prospects: The congressionally mandated study of educational growth and opportunity interim report: Language minority and limited English proficient children. (1995). Washington, DC: U.S. Department of Education.

Raoufi, S. (1981). The children of guest-workers in the Federal Republic of Germany: Maladjustment and its effects on academic performance. In J. Edwards (Ed.), *Educating immigrants* (pp. 137–157). New York: St. Martin's Press.

Ravem, R. (1968). Language acquisition in a second language environment. *International Review of Applied Linguistics, 6*, 165–185.

Ravem, R. (1974). The development of *Wh-* questions in first and second language learners. In J. Richards (Ed.), *Error analysis* (pp. 134–155). London: Longman.

Richards, J. C., & Rodgers, T. S. (1986). *Approaches and methods in language teaching*. Cambridge, UK: Cambridge University Press.

Rivera, K. (1988). Not "either/or" but "and": Literacy for non-English speakers. *Focus on Basics, 1*(3/4), 1–3.

Robson, B. (1982). Hmong literacy, formal education and their efforts on performance in the ESL class. In B. Downing & O. Douglas (Eds.), *The Hmong in the West*. Minneapolis, MN: University of Minnesota, Center for Urban and Regional Affairs.

Roosens, E. (1989). Cultural ecology and achievement motivation: Ethnic minority youngsters in the Belgian system. In L. Eldering & J. Kloprogge (Eds.), *Different cultures, same school: Ethnic minority children in Europe* (pp. 85–106). Amsterdam: Swets & Zeitlinger.

Rumbaut, R. (1990). *Immigrant students in California public schools: A summary of current knowledge* (Report #11). Baltimore, MD: Center for Research on Effective Schooling for Disadvantaged Students.

Rumberger, R. W. (1998). California LEP enrollment growth rate falls. *UC LMRI Newsletter, 8,* 1–2.

Sarason, S. B. (1996). *Revisiting the culture of the school and the problem of change.* New York: Teachers College Press.

Selinker, L. (1972). Interlanguage. *International Review of Applied Linguistics, 10,* 209–231.

Selinker, L. (1992). *Rediscovering interlanguage.* London: Longman.

Shamash, Y. (1990). Learning in translation: Beyond language experience in ESL. *Voices, 2*(2), 71–75.

Siguan, M. (1983). *Lenguas y educación en el ámbito del estado español.* Barcelona: Publicaciones de la Universidad de Barcelona.

Simon, R. (1986). Empowerment as a pedagogy of possibility. *Language Arts, 64,* 370–382.

Skehan, P. (1989). *Individual differences in second-language learning.* London: Edward Arnold.

Skutnabb-Kangas, T. (1981). *Bilingualism or not: The education of minorities.* Clevedon, UK: Multilingual Matters.

Skutnabb-Kangas, T., & Cummins, J. (Eds.). (1988). *Minority education: From shame to struggle.* Clevedon, UK: Multilingual Matters.

Smolicz, J. J. (1986). National language policy in the Philippines. In B. Spolsky (Ed.), *Language and education in multilingual settings* (pp. 96–116). San Diego, CA: College-Hill Press.

Spolsky, B. (1986). *Language and education in multilingual settings.* San Diego, CA: College-Hill Press.

Spolsky, B. (1989). *Conditions for second language learning.* Oxford, UK: Oxford University Press.

Srivastava, R. N. (1988). Societal bilingualism and bilingual education: A study of the Indian situation. In C. B. Paulston (Ed.), *International handbook of bilingualism and bilingual education* (pp. 247–274). New York: Greenwood.

Swain, M. (1985). Communicative competence: Some roles of comprehensible input and comprehensible output in its development. In S. M. Gass & C. G. Madden (Eds.), *Input in second language acquisition* (pp. 235–253). Rowley, MA: Newbury House.

Swerdlik, M. E. (1992). Review of the Gates-MacGinitie Reading Tests Third Edition. In J. J. Kramer & J. C. Conoley (Eds.), *The eleventh mental measurements yearbook* (pp. 350–354). Lincoln, NB: Buros Institute of Mental Measurement.

Terrell, T. D. (1977). A natural approach to second language acquisition and learning. *Modern Language Journal, 61,* 325–336.

TESOL. (1997). *ESL standards for Pre-K–12 students.* Alexandria, VA: Author.

Thompson, L., Fleming, M., & Byram, M. (1996). Language and language policy in Britain. In M. Herriman & B. Burnaby (Eds.), *Language policies in English-dominant countries* (pp. 99–121). Clevedon, UK: Multilingual Matters.

Tollefson, J. W. (1991). *Planning language, planning inequality: Language policy in the community*. London: Longman.

Tollefson, J. W. (Ed.). (1995). *Power and inequality in language education*. Cambridge, UK: Cambridge University Press.

Tosi, A. (1989). *Immigration and bilingual education*. Oxford, UK: Pergamon Press.

Valdés, G. (1996). *Con respeto: Bridging the distances between culturally diverse families and schools: An ethnographic portrait*. New York: Teachers College Press.

Valdés, G. (1999). Incipient bilingualism and the development of English language writing abilities in the secondary school. In C. J. Faltis & P. M. Wolfe (Eds.), *So much to say: Adolescents, bilingualism and ESL in the secondary school* (pp. 138–175). New York: Teachers College Press.

Valdés, G., & Sanders, P. A. (1998). Latino ESL students and the development of writing abilities. In C. R. Cooper & L. Odell (Eds.), *Evaluating writing* (pp. 249–278). Urbana, IL: National Council of Teachers of English.

Wallace, C. (1992). Critical literacy awareness in the EFL classroom. In N. Fairclough (Ed.), *Critical language awareness* (pp. 59–92). London: Longman.

Willis, P. (1977). *Learning to labor: How working class kids get working class jobs*. New York: Columbia University Press.

Wong Fillmore, L. (1982). Language minority students and school participation: What kind of English is needed? *Journal of Education, 164*(2), 143–156.

Wong Fillmore, L. (1985). When does teacher talk work as input. In S. Gass & C. Madden (Eds.), *Input in second language acquisition* (pp. 17–50). Rowley, MA: Newbury.

Wong Fillmore, L. (1991). Second language learning in children: A model of language learning in social context. In E. Bialystok (Ed.), *Language processing in bilingual children* (pp. 49–69). Cambridge, UK: Cambridge University Press.

Wong Fillmore, L. (1992). Learning a language from learners. In C. Kramsch & S. McConnell-Ginet (Eds.), *Text and context: Cross-disciplinary perspectives on language study* (pp. 46–66). Lexington, MA: Heath.

Index

About the Author

Guadalupe Valdés is Professor of Education and Professor of Spanish and Portuguese at Stanford University. A native of the U.S.–Mexican border, she commuted across the border from Juárez, Mexico, to attend Loretto Academy in El Paso, Texas, during her elementary and high school years. She then left the border area to reside in Florida for 8 years. Dr. Valdés received both her master's degree and doctorate in Spanish from Florida State University in 1968 and 1972, respectively.

After completing her doctorate, Valdés returned to the border area, where she joined the faculty of New Mexico State University. She remained in New Mexico for 14 years, during which time she carried out research on the English–Spanish bilingualism of Mexican-origin residents of the area. In 1986, she left the border area for northern California, where she became a member of the faculty of the School of Education at the University of California–Berkeley, where she remained until 1992.

Most of Valdés's work is concerned with discovering and describing how two languages are developed, used, and maintained by individuals who become bilingual in immigrant communities. Her research has described language use in bilingual settings (e.g. code-switching, language accommodation, language maintenance, and the use of language in school and courtroom settings) and the application of the information obtained from such descriptions to the educational context. Valdés's recent work includes *Bilingualism and Testing: A Special Case of Bias* (Ablex, 1994), *Con respecto: Bridging the Distances Between Families and Schools* (Teachers College Press, 1996), "Nonnative English Speakers: Language Bigotry in English Mainstream Classrooms" (*ADFL Bulletin*, 1999), "Chicano Spanish: The Problem of the 'Underdeveloped' Code in Bilingual Repertoires" (*Modern Language Journal*, 1998), "Bilinguals and Bilingualism: Language Policy in an Anti-Immigrant Age" (*International Journal of the Sociology of Language*, 1997), and "Dual Language Immersion Programs: A Cautionary Note Concerning the Education of Language Minority Students" (*Harvard Educational Review, 1997).*